THE ADVENTURE WITHIN

Why successful professionals still feel stuck and how to purposefully rekindle your craving for adventure.

Published by

KICK&CO SYNERGY LTD
www.kicknco.com

info@kickandcosynergy.com

ISBN 979-8-9912464-1-5

Printed in the USA

FOREWORD

I have had the unique privilege of watching Jim's transformation—not just as a leader, but as a man deeply committed to living within purpose.

For over two decades, he thrived in Corporate America, traveling constantly, taking on high-profile roles, and achieving success by every conventional measure.

As a sales manager and global consultant, he worked with some of the biggest names, led major projects, and navigated complex corporate structures.

From the outside, he seemed like the perfect role model—an accomplished career, financially secure, and a strong family life.

Even though I couldn't quite define it at the time, I knew that all was not as it should be.

Jim was busy, but not fulfilled.

I remember the late nights when he would return home exhausted, drained from back-to-back meetings, deadlines, targets, and responsibilities. And yet, before he could fully rest, he was already preparing for his next flight, another work engagement, another packed schedule. Work always came first. It was his way of life.

Jim was searching for something more—something deeper than just worldly success. Over time, that feeling became impossible to ignore. It wasn't that he lacked gratitude for what he had; rather, he realized that the path he was on was no longer aligned with the person he wanted to be.

Jim's transition from a high-performing professional to a purpose-driven leader wasn't immediate. It was a gradual, intentional journey that took years of deep reflection, courage, and, most importantly, the willingness to step away from the safety of past endeavors.

But the more he leaned into this journey, the clearer it became that he was being called to something greater. Something beyond him.

That calling led to the creation of **Conjunction Leadership,** a company Jim built six years ago not just on conventional leadership theories but on real, lived experiences.

Through this work, Jim helps other leaders navigate the very transition he faced—shifting from a life of reactive living to one of self-authored fulfillment.

Jim's mission is simple yet profound: to help individuals break free from old paradigms that keep them feeling stuck and move toward a life of meaning where they reach their fullest potential.

What I admire most about Jim is that he doesn't just teach these principles—he lives them. The insights in *The Adventure Within* are not abstract concepts; they are hard-earned truths.

I have witnessed his relentless commitment to refining this book, ensuring that every sentence, paragraph, and chapter reflects the depth of his journey and experiences. I'm happy to have assisted where necessary, too.

There are many leadership and self-help books out there, but *The Adventure Within* is different. It is not a diagnostic and prescriptive book filled with generic advice, nor is it a step-by-step guide promising overnight success. Instead, it is an invitation—an adventure in itself.

Jim has woven together real-life stories and deeply personal insights that will resonate with anyone who has ever felt stuck in their leadership journey.

What makes this book truly special is how it speaks directly to the reader. As you journey through its pages, you will see yourself in the characters. You will recognize the patterns of behavior that have kept you tethered to a life of safety rather than purpose. And most importantly, you will gain clarity not just about what is missing, but about what steps you need to take to bridge that gap.

I believe this book will challenge you in the best possible way. It will prompt you to reflect on your own journey, to ask yourself difficult but necessary questions, and to consider whether the life you are living is the one you were meant for. It is a book that does not allow you to remain passive. It calls you to action.

As Jim's wife, I have had a front-row seat to his transformation, and I can say with certainty that he is a different man today than he was when we first met. He is more present, more intentional, and more fulfilled— not just in his work, but in every area of life.

If you are reading this book, I believe you are on the path of your own transformation. You may have already achieved success, but you sense that there is more waiting for you—more meaning, more impact, more fulfillment.

The Adventure Within is your guide to uncovering that next chapter.

This is not just another leadership book to read and set aside; it will stay with you long after you turn the last page. It will challenge you, encourage you, and most importantly, empower you to step into the adventure that is waiting for you on the other side of safety.

I wholeheartedly recommend *The Adventure Within:* A transformational journey waiting to be embraced.

– **Nicole Bishop**

ABSTRACT

High-achievers often appear to have it all—material success, recognition, and influence. Yet, beneath this shiny exterior lies a silent tension: a worrying sense of emptiness, a disconnection from the passion and drive that once fueled their ascent.

The Adventure Within unravels this paradox, revealing why most accomplished professionals feel stuck.

The book reveals how clinging to the safe habits that built their success prevents them from embracing the purposeful actions needed to reach where they were intended to be.

This transformative book is for leaders who recognize the need for growth but fear the uncertainty it demands. It challenges readers to confront the discomfort of change and venture beyond the identities that have defined them over time.

Divided into three parts and ten chapters, *The Adventure Within* leads readers on a profound journey of self-discovery. It examines the learned behaviors that shape our lives, uncovers what truly sparks vitality, and offers practical steps to reignite a sense of purpose.

Through vivid case studies and relatable archetypes, readers will see themselves in these stories, finding both clarity and courage to reclaim the adventurous spirit they once had as children.

Practical, inspiring, and deeply personal, *The Adventure Within* is a must-have, serving as a blueprint for both accomplished and aspiring leaders ready to move beyond safety to discover a life of meaning, purpose, and fulfillment.

PROLOGUE

The smell of freshly baled straw. The humid heat of a late summer afternoon. Laughs and giggles as my siblings, cousins and I invested hours upon hours into creating the ideal fort out of straw bales in my family's barn loft. We would get lost for hours at a time in our play until my parents called us back inside for dinner.

For me, an Indiana farm kid, straw forts and country adventures defined my sense of play and creativity. Looking back on that play, it was much more than just recreation; it was a re-creation. I was becoming something new in play. I was in charge of my destiny. Responsible for learning (often through making mistakes and realizing imperfections). I was loving the relationships I was building as we created together. As an adult, I can look back and understand what was happening in that haymow that went far beyond the forts we built. I can see now that I was learning to cooperate with others, resolve disagreements, make peace, and even understand how the laws of physics worked in everyday life. (How high can you stack these imperfectly sized bales before they collapse?) What I thought was play was actually education and a re-creation of the kid in me toward a more defined existence as a human.

As a kid, what was your sense of play and creativity? Climbing trees, building Lego, stomping in a creek? Whatever it was, do you remember how effortless it felt? You likely played for hours and hours without feeling bored or tired. Sure, your body might have tired eventually, but your sense of adventure was propelling you forward. As a kid, your sense of learning and growth were uninhibited. But let me ask: Where is that sense of adventure in your life today?

For me, it was a slow decline that took years to realize where things seemed to go wrong. Over time, play was slowly replaced with duty. Recreation seemed selfish and indulgent, so I replaced it with earning a living and providing for my family. Rather than for the mere fun of it, learning was geared towards acquiring the requisite skills to get ahead in my work and was done with careful curation and prescription to prove my worth.

I have to admit, though, it was all done with good intent. The responsible adult in me, who wanted more for my kids than I had, decided to work harder, be smarter, and become more likable than anyone else. That sense of creativity from the haymow was replaced with learning how to play by the rules of corporate America to get ahead, earn more, and become more "valuable" to my employer, de-risking the chances of being impacted by the next round of restructuring.

Because I was evaluating myself by my intent—to provide for and protect my family—I didn't even realize I had shifted into safety mode, seemingly reacting to the world around me. My wife and I were blessed with our fifth child, and I was traveling extensively for work, which took me away from my family. These blessings we had so desired seemed like the very same things that were keeping me from advancing in my career. "If only I could travel more," I caught myself thinking one night alone in my hotel room. I tried to push onward for another three years. Yet slowly this sense of growing languishing overtook me, and I realized something had changed.

My sense of adventure, replaced with a sense of playing it safe. My sense of creativity, displaced by reacting to the perceived rules around me. And the joy that I had been pursuing eluded me and was eventually replaced by an overwhelming sense of dread and disappointment every time I was passed up for another promotion—my shot at securing even more "safety" in my corporate role. I longed to be a kid again in the adventure of the hayloft, creating, relating, learning, and fully in charge of my decisions.

I had a decision to make. I could choose to act, or I could sit by waiting to be acted on. I could press forward with hard work on myself or regress into the growing sense of powerlessness I felt by existing in the proverbial box as I quite literally earned a paycheck by working in a cubicle, sitting in an airplane or in lonely hotel rooms—all boxes in their own right. I couldn't remain complacent any longer. Time seemed of the essence. I wasn't getting any younger. My kids needed me. My wife needed me. And to be honest, I could tell the world needed something I had to offer, even if I wasn't quite sure what that was yet.

So, I pursued the long and winding path to the greatest adventure of my life. *The Adventure Within*. The adventure to learn about how I had developed these survival instincts that had helped me to adeptly navigate school, earn a graduate degree, raise five kids with my wife, and succeed for 20 years in Corporate America, advancing in title and responsibility. I was successful by all outside measures. But internally I felt like a mess. If life is about living, why did I feel like I was barely hanging on? The life I was living, the life I had worked so hard for, felt incongruent with the yearnings of my soul. There had to be more. But does someone with seemingly everything they set out to acquire have the audacity to ask, "Is there more?" when so many have so little around the world? Why couldn't I just be content, and grateful for the things I already have?

The examples that follow in *"The Adventure Within"* are examples based on the many hundreds of clients who have placed their trust in me to help them navigate these same waters. The characters are fictitious, but the examples in their lives are not. These are real examples, conversations, and emotions. These are not just based on my clients but also my personal experience of living this tension between being anchored in safety and simultaneously being pulled toward more meaning, more purpose, and more legacy in my own life.

My hope for you is that you can see yourself in some of the examples that follow. And that you will choose to take action on the greatest adventure in your life—*The Adventure Within*.

As you'll see from these clients, it's not easy. It requires courage. Courage to step into some of the painful experiences in your past and extract meaning and understanding. It requires emotional intelligence. For far too long, your emotions have been bossing you around. And now, it's time that you put a name to them so you can make them your servants, not your masters. This journey requires that you let go. You need to let go of some of the safety behaviors that got you where you're at for some of the purposeful behaviors that will propel you to go forward to where you were intended to be. Unfortunately, some of you along this path will decide the journey is much too difficult. And you will turn back. You will allow the anchor of safety to hold you back only to never realize the true joy and sense of purpose that is on the other side. Both paths are hard. But *The Adventure Within* is the hard path that leads to breakthrough.

My hope for you is that you will choose the path that leads to the freedom you've been trying to achieve on your own all along. It is the greatest adventure of your lifetime.

Bon voyage as we embark on *The Adventure Within.*

CONTENTS

· CHAPTER ONE ·

THE NAGGING VOICE WITHIN

Susan

Susan Michael, the epitome of entrepreneurial success, stood at the peak of her career. She had become one of the wealthiest women in Seattle. She had more money than she knew what to do with it. Yet despite her immense wealth and success, there was a persistent worry, a sense of being stuck. At age 49, squarely in midlife, Susan began questioning her true purpose and legacy.

Susan's journey wasn't paved in gold, nor was it the smoothest. Rising from a financially strained relationship 18 years ago, she built her first business from the ground up, owing her success to her fierce independence and tireless work ethic. Her innate ability to organize and control everything had helped her amass all this wealth. The more she achieved, the more she felt the need to organize and ultimately control—a hunger born from a fear of losing what she'd labored so hard to build—her wealth and status, which were tangible proof of her success in life.

However, if there was one thing Susan feared losing more than her material possessions, it was her relationships and the sense of belonging to those whom she cared for the most. But Susan would soon find out that she had begun to overcompensate in subsequent relationships. She never argued, rarely disagreed, yet was able to steer conversations, ensuring decisions aligned with her vision. She avoided any perception of causing conflict with others.

The bane of Susan's distress became evident with her acquisition of Westland Clothing. Here, she encountered a stark contrast to her leadership approach—Paul Hacker, the founder. Paul was an intuitive creative who lived and breathed design. However, his business practices were as chaotic as his ideas. And so, concerned about Westland's well-being, Susan sought out leadership coaching for Paul.

This was the beginning of our journey together.

While Paul was indeed burned out from work and sought creative freedom, it was clear that Susan needed coaching just as much. She genuinely cared for him, but her incessant inquiries about his progress revealed an underlying need for control. She wanted me to assess Paul's work without her direct involvement, subtly guiding me to criticize his efforts and coach him to be more organized and in control.

Susan's employees, on the other hand, adored her. They saw a dedicated and thoughtful leader, not a dictator. However, her frustration with their perceived inadequacies manifested in a peculiar way. Rather than offering direct criticism, she would express mild disappointment and then take over the project herself. Susan found herself overworked and often feeling underappreciated.

Her friends and family, who had no professional relationship with Susan, saw a different side of her. On the surface, she appeared kind and generous to them, yet most admitted she seemed to expect something in return for her generosity.

The inevitable happened.

Unable to function optimally under the weight of Susan's expectations, Paul left Westland Clothing, selling his shares of the company he'd founded. He felt undermined. Susan, who loved to be in control over every aspect of her life, ended up pushing away an invaluable asset and felt very out of control.

Watching Paul walk away without being able to do anything about it kept her up at night. The emptiness she felt wasn't a lack of achievement but a hollowness born of isolation. "I was driving into the office today," Susan admitted to me. "And all I could think was, 'I'm tired of leading like this; building people up only to watch them quit.' Especially someone like Paul, after all I did for him. I keep feeling like leadership should be easier than this. Am I a bad leader?"

I explained the importance of self-discovery. "Before we look at changing other people, are you first willing to change yourself?" I inquired.

"I think I am," she said hesitantly.

"The first step is to understand what got you to where you're at," I replied. "To go forward, sometimes we need to learn from the past. I'll give you a worksheet that will guide you in some personal reflection. Take your time when filling it out," I replied. "When is our next appointment?"

"In two weeks, Jim," she confirmed.

Scott

Scott Ford, a seasoned accountant working at Zine Group Ltd., an oil and gas company, had spent the last 10 years climbing the corporate ladder. At 55, he had risen to become the Chief Financial Officer (CFO), the highest rung in his profession, after joining as a junior accountant.

Scott's life mirrored his personality—a religious faithful bound by strict doctrines, a workaholic, and a self-proclaimed family man. His success was based on hard work (which meant he had to work overtime and keep late nights), a keen eye for detail, and a strong dislike for making trouble, or at the very least, getting people upset. He seemed to thrive on external validation.

Promotions came, not because Scott desperately sought them, but because he was technically competent and had a reputation as a "people person." The promotion to CFO was a natural step, a reward for years of loyal service and precise accounting skills. Yet, as he made this move, he couldn't fathom eventually becoming the number one person at Zine Group, the CEO. His comfort zone was being a subject matter expert, not the broader organizational and leadership roles that came with his new position or any future role that would take him out of his area of expertise.

With this CFO role came an increased requirement for understanding the functioning of Zine Group. He was now responsible for more people and therefore a lot more complexity. He had more corporate functions, more investment relations, and more boardroom meetings. Indeed, these were foreign lands, far from his true training or expertise. Candidly, he knew these responsibilities stretched his competence and challenged his self-image.

He loved to hear "good job" from his superiors and those he worked with.

Zine Group required a compulsory leadership 360 evaluation for all executive leaders. It was meant to give helpful feedback. But the potential for others to see his weaknesses meant it was a source of stress for Scott.

Determined to prove the feedback wrong, Scott reached out to me.

"I need to show them that I have a voice," he said, his eyes filled with determination. "I need to prove to them that I can make Zine Group better."

"Why?" I asked.

"Because they will think I'm unqualified for this role if I don't change," remarked Scott.

Early in our coaching relationship, I noticed a pattern. Scott had a hard time "taking responsibility for his own destiny." He seemed to rely on me for guidance and validation. He was constantly seeking reassurance, asking if he was doing the right thing and if people liked him. His fear of rejection was palpable.

I challenged him to step into his own power by anchoring him in the outcomes he wanted to achieve. "My coaching job is to hear, reflect, and help you align with your goals," I would always say.

Then, I inquired further, "What goals do you want to achieve?"

And almost as a foreshadowing of things to come, Scott said, "To be successful." Yet, he had no real understanding of what success meant except for referring to the fact that it meant meeting everyone else's expectations and responding favorably to the 360 feedback he'd received.

Scott admitted that he preferred to remain in the background, avoiding conflict. But this passive approach was leading to resentment and bitterness. Resentment from the peers who expected him to step up to the new role and bitterness within himself as he questioned his capabilities. He preferred to vent to me during our sessions, sharing exhaustive explanations and justifications for why things were the way they were. Rarely did he acknowledge his responsibility in the situation or see it as something that was dynamic and able to change.

Scott shared a recent incident with Jane Witham, an internal tax auditor and new direct report to Scott, who had failed to complete a rather simple task he had assigned her. While he was disappointed, he hadn't confronted her. He feared that expressing his dissatisfaction would damage their relationship. He locked his frustration inside, building resentment and anger along the way, and misconstrued Jane's lack of completion as disrespect for his leadership.

I challenged him to confront his fear of conflict and a need to please everyone. "What is your reluctance to speak up costing you as a leader?

"I'm not sure it's costing me anything," Scott said in defense.

What he couldn't see yet was that the growing sense of frustration and resentment he carried was the nagging voice inside of him. It was screaming for peace. "What you tolerate is how you teach people to treat you," I summarized, as we concluded one of our conversations. Scott was clearly not able to discern his growing

> **What you tolerate teaches people how to treat you.**

frustration and nagging sense of imposter syndrome in his new job as a call from within to change.

Scott's relationship with his CEO, Liz Curry, grew strained as well. Liz was a decisive and assertive leader who had built her leadership in many organizations where she was not the industry expert. She was known as the leader who surrounded herself with even stronger leaders and who could turn a company around in just a few quarters. Liz, who had handpicked Scott to be CFO, was growing frustrated with Scott's lack of assertiveness and was silently second-guessing her decision to promote him. She needed someone who could contribute their own insights and challenge her ideas to help the business advance. She had no time for another "Yes Man" in her lineup.

Realizing that his reputation was at risk, Scott sought my advice. "How do I get my voice heard? How do I become the leader Liz wants me to be?" he asked. "I owe it to her to be successful and to help her be successful. She gave me this promotion."

He had dedicated his life to Zine Group, sacrificing family time—a value he held strongly—and well-being, and now he might lose it all. While he sensed his professional accomplishments were at risk, he feared the loss of respect from his family even more—for they had borne the brunt of his dedication to this company and knew the pain of the sacrifices he made for Zine the most.

As we were about to wrap up our first appointment, I offered an insight for him to reflect on: "When you put others before yourself all the time, you avoid tension—external conflict. However, an internal conflict arises. Suffocating yourself is not the appropriate thing to do. You need to bring things to the surface to arrive at a win-win solution. You must be more vulnerable and direct to find belonging and meaning," I explained.

I could tell this comment sat hard with Scott. He wasn't yet ready to accept the fact that he was a pushover, but, indeed, something had struck a chord with him. I was eager to dive in further in our next conversation. Yet I was unsure if Scott would respond as favorably to the challenges before him or my direct approach with him.

Mike

Mike Flair, now 56, was the CEO of First Lead Technology Ltd., an automobile company. Born and raised in California, Mike had a rocky childhood. He didn't have a supportive network growing up; his father was a crude mechanical engineer, who worked with his hands but was not very successful. From his father, Mike learned the value of hands-on work and, more importantly, how to learn. "If I continue to learn, I'll get ahead," Mike thought to himself. He did, rising from a lab attendant to the role of CEO.

Mike started working at First Lead Technology Ltd. as a high school student. He took on odd jobs, doing anything that needed to be done and fixing mechanical stuff. His innate curiosity and ability to learn quickly made him stand out.

After graduating high school, Mike secured a full-time position at the company. He tarried in the workshop, handling mechanical tasks, fixing things, and learning the chemistry and mechanics of cars. He became quite knowledgeable in the field, gaining a deep understanding of the company's products and processes. Mike's intellectual prowess didn't go unnoticed. One day he came up with a new solution that significantly improved the ease of computer applications in vehicles. His solution caught the attention of the company's leaders.

Recognizing Mike's potential, the leadership at First Lead Technology Ltd. offered to pay for his college education, with the condition that he would return to the company after graduation. Mike agreed and applied to study mechanical engineering at the California Institute of Technology. There, he expanded his knowledge, met new mentors, and further honed his skills.

Four years later, Mike returned to the company as a highly educated and skilled professional. He was promoted to full employee and quickly climbed the ranks. Along the way, he met his wife, Lily Jones, who was also an employee at the company.

Hard work and intellectual achievement characterized Mike's progress in the company. He moved through various divisions, eventually becoming the president and, later, the CEO of First Lead Technology Ltd. He'd developed a reputation and a sense of pride in it as an independent problem solver. It was evident that this was part of his core identity.

As CEO, Mike's tendency to solve problems himself became more pronounced. When conflicts or issues arose among the staff, his immediate response was to dive in and outline the solution. He believed that he knew everything there was to know about the organization, given his long history with the company. If there was a problem, Mike preferred to step in and tell people what to do, often without considering their perspectives or helping them develop their problem-solving skills.

When the innovation department faced a significant challenge—the department's pipeline was not producing enough innovative ideas—Mike's response was to organize a global innovation summit, inviting a cast of global employees to participate and learn how to implement the solution he'd designed. He believed that only he knew the right people and the necessary steps to address the issue. He sent the invite, created the agenda, and facilitated the meeting.

This approach reflected his belief that he needed to have all the answers and direct the company's efforts.

As Mike settled into his role as CEO, he began to feel the weight of his responsibilities. His calendar was packed with meetings and problem-solving sessions. He was constantly organizing agendas and providing answers to everyone who seemed to have a problem and sometimes even to those who didn't. This left him with little time for himself, leading to anxiety and burnout. Exhausted, he admitted that he worried that he wasn't meeting the board's expectations of developing the strategic plan for the company to grow in what was predicted to be a tight upcoming economy. Inside, he worried he wasn't going to be able to meet their demanding expectations.

The problems Mike faced as CEO were more complex than those he had encountered as an expert in the Chassis and Transmission Lab. He now had to consider broader issues, such as government regulations, economic conditions, and strategic planning. Mike struggled with the realization that he couldn't control everything and that he needed to rely on others to navigate these complexities. He struggled even more to admit his fear of not being able to know enough in each of those areas to make the decisions the board expected him to make.

Mike would usually retreat within himself to come up with the answer. He rarely relied on others, though he had good relationships with most of his direct reports. This prevented other leaders from figuring out solutions on their own, and Mike found himself trapped in a quandary. "If I don't tell them what to do, they'll get it wrong. If I do tell them what to do, they don't take ownership, and I have to do it all over again. What am I to do?" He was rapidly burning himself out trying to manage every detail while also trying to lead the business as its CEO.

Mike's personal life also added to his stress. His children, Katie (28), Hall (25), and Noah (19), had made choices that Mike didn't agree with and Mike felt like he was bearing the consequences of their actions. He silently shamed himself for the missed opportunities he'd overlooked in their childhood to help them make wise choices. He regretted so much of the time he spent at the office. This situation was a growing source of frustration for him. He wanted to guide his now-adult children and tell them what to do, but he knew they had the right to make their own decisions.

That frustration, combined with his persistent burnout as CEO, was how he became my client.

"The sooner you realize you cannot know enough to be in control of everything, the better off you will be," were my final words as we concluded our first meeting.

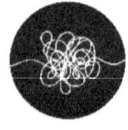

· CHAPTER TWO ·

THE FALSE BIND

Susan: Control or Lose Control

After reviewing the 360 assessment we had just conducted, something became apparent. Though she'd spent a lifetime trying to dismiss it, Susan Michael's regimented childhood influenced her view of the world more than she cared to admit.

"What informed your perspective of leadership?" I asked Susan as we began the session.

"My dad was my earliest influence," she replied. "I looked up to him as a child and wanted to be like him when I grew up."

Her father, Steve Michael, a decorated US Army officer, ran the household with a firm hand. Curfews were strict, and weekends were for educational pursuits, not socializing. Vacations, higher education, and even course selections were all dictated. Questioning his decisions was met with a cold rebuke, leaving young Susan feeling stifled and helpless, emotions she didn't like to admit out loud.

This environment shaped her personality. Not entirely aware of her early leadership choices, she recognized that early in her journey she had subliminally decided never to make others feel as she had growing up and therefore, would never enact such a level of control on anyone. However, the yearning for her parents' approval meant she had to learn to accept and bend to her father's iron control. Subconsciously, she began to internalize her father's behavior, agreeing not to be like him when interacting with others but also mistaking his desire to control for his protective love for her as a growing child. Control, she reasoned, must be the key to earning others' affection. And likewise, though less apparent to her, being out of control could be a reason to lose affection.

This dynamic also played out in her first college relationship. She sought out and found a man with similar controlling tendencies, just like her father. In this relationship, she found her self-esteem slowly eroding. He'd express dissatisfaction with her appearance, suggesting "improvements" through aggressive diet plans and gym routines. Slowly, Susan's love for her own body gave way to a relentless pursuit of his ideal as she started to view her body through his critical lens, nursing self-hatred under the guise of self-improvement. That experience reinforced her belief that control and discipline were necessary ingredients to maintain love and connection.

Still, Susan feared hurting others with her desire to be in control. She's been labelled "bossy" one too many times in her youth, and that earned her the opposite of the affection she sought. She chose to live differently. She'd shower those around her with affection and kindness, sometimes to the extreme. Though she wasn't aware of it, she was doing so hoping to create a sense of obligation to her, wishing that they would reciprocate with the appreciation and love she expected. Disagreements were non-existent, replaced by agreeableness. Instead of barking orders, she learned to rely on "less harmful" questions that steered conversations from conflicts of any sorts, of any degree. Her true feelings and frustrations were buried deep, as she feared the disapproval that might result from expressing them. On the surface she appeared to be rather compliant—a behavior she likely cultivated from dealing with her ex-boyfriend and father—but brewing underneath was a feeling of resentment that led to feeling out of control—a feeling that Susan loathed more than anything.

For most of her adult life, this personality she expressed brought her much success. She was a successful entrepreneur who had tried her hand at several businesses. She was involved in and maintained firm controls on them all despite each having their own president.

In just a few coaching sessions, Susan had developed a transformative insight. She realized that her controlling tendencies were rooted in her childhood experiences. As a child, she had learned to equate the level of control she exhibited with the amount of respect and approval she earned—cheap substitutes for the love and belonging she coveted the most.

"The drive you possess, the ambition, the will to win, the competitive spirit, the tenacity to get ahead and achieve success—those are gifts of the controlling nature. They're the very things that motivated you to build your empire," I made her aware. "However, when used to dominate people, it isolates you, pushing away the very connections you genuinely desire. The feedback from your team seems to be in contradiction. They see you doing what you can to be seen as "non-controlling" by showering them with praise and kindness and sometimes gifts. In a sense, it's almost like you become passive-aggressive to remain in control while attempting to minimize the negativity you associate with feeling controlled.

"You could not suppress the controlling nature within you, but realizing its detriments, you became artificially nice to them, essentially living as a double agent."

Susan began to see how her present identity had been shaped by her experiences and how her controlling nature was affecting her relationships. "I need to reflect on my relationships and speak with the people I care about," she said. "I don't want to continue living like this. It's eating me up, and it's killing my relationships."

As we concluded our second session, I knew that Susan was on the path to understanding herself and breaking free from the controlling patterns that had defined her life. "The key to learning new behaviors is to first disrupt the things we've subconsciously learned to provide our sense of self with stability, meaning, and safety. To grow, we must first disrupt," I shared with her finally.

> **To grow, we must first disrupt.**

Scott: Comply or Be Rejected

Scott recalled the linear structure of his upbringing when I asked how he defined good leadership. "It's about adhering to structure, routine, and order," he said. "Sundays were reserved for church service, Bible study, and youth group meetings," I remembered him saying. His devout parents, Martha and William Ford, viewed the world through a lens of religious dogma. "Dead to the flesh, alive in the Spirit," they would often proclaim, emphasizing obedience as the cornerstone of the Christian faith. Questioning authority, especially divinely ordained authority, was considered rebelliousness to God. You need to "love your neighbor as yourself." Scott learned to adhere to and build a community at the same time. His community was his place of safety, a place he felt loved. He enjoyed supporting others and found meaning and safety in accepting the structures and boundaries.

As a student within the walls of his high school, Scott thrived. He excelled essentially because he learned what his teachers wanted. He promptly submitted classwork and assignments, completed all the extra credits, and came in for extra help after hours. Scott knew exactly how much to study and how to avoid distractions that would keep him from earning the respect, praise, and affirmation of the educational staff. He had learned to use the teachers' expectations to create boundaries and rules to garner him the success and respect he coveted.

The concept of community, instilled by his parents, became paramount to Scott. Belonging to a group, be it his family, his church youth group, or the school's sports team, became his source of validation. He wasn't outstanding on his high school football team, at least not enough to make the first team, but his coach recognized his attitude. "Attitude trumps talent," Scott recalled his coach saying, pointing at him as he addressed the team before practice sessions. Though not expressed directly, Scott interpreted this to mean that too much aggression could be construed as defiance or a bad attitude, so he fell nicely in line with the coach and his direction.

He loved being accepted and reveled in the feeling of being part of something bigger than himself. Stepping out of line, voicing dissent, or challenging the status quo risked being rejected, the very thing he feared most.

When Scott joined Zine Group as a junior accountant, his unwavering obedience was initially perceived as a positive trait. He followed instructions meticulously, rarely questioned procedures, and readily absorbed the company's culture. Senior colleagues commended his work ethic and his willingness to go the extra mile.

He often stayed late to complete tasks without a murmur of complaint. His attention to making sure there were no mistakes earned him a favorable reputation in the tightly controlled discipline of accounting.

However, as Scott rose through the ranks, he struggled with delegation, fearing that assigning tasks would be seen as a lack of his own commitment. Secondary to that, he also hated telling people they had opportunities to improve, seeing it as a chastisement of their character rather than an opportunity to become better in their craft. He avoided conflict, even where necessary for the benefit of the project, choosing to appease colleagues and those in authority rather than advocate for the best course of action. This led to missed opportunities to showcase his own expertise, strategic thinking, and any sense of individual creativity.

As a junior accountant, he had dreamed of climbing the corporate ladder and achieving a position of power and respect. Yet, this ambition was often in conflict with his fear of rejection and his need for approval. To be seen as a "good soldier," he downplayed his own ideas, hesitant to challenge the decisions of his superiors. He became a master of reading moods, adjusting his own opinions to align with what he perceived the leadership wanted to hear. As he rose in his career, this "concern for others" was seen as a valuable trait when leading teams, as he often helped those under his influence feel valued and built systems and structures around their needs—while disregarding his own. "Scott's a great team player" appeared on one of his early performance reviews, and he wore it as a badge of honor for his career. As a leader, he was always eager to see his team's engagement score. The higher the score, the more the team liked his leadership, he would conclude. Therefore, he was doing a good job as a leader.

Yet, this lack of assertiveness frustrated his colleagues, particularly those who saw his potential. They recognized his sharp financial mind and his dedication to the company, but they were left yearning for a leader who could offer fresh perspectives and challenge the status quo. As opportunities for advancement arose, Scott often found himself passed over for those who were more vocal and demonstrated greater initiative.

The most significant consequence of Scott's compliance may have been the erosion of his personal life. Family time, a value he held dear, was sacrificed at the altar of professional advancement. He missed birthdays and school plays, prioritizing late nights at the office over building memories with his wife and children. While his family initially supported his career aspirations, the cracks began to show as his physical and emotional absence became increasingly evident. "I think something is happening, and you are refusing to tell me. Instead, you are immersing yourself in work as though you are running from an enemy," his wife, Jessica, would confront him, concerned.

As Scott shared his experiences, I could observe how much stress and pressure he was under. I listened intently before responding. "There are benefits to being agreeable that have worked for you until now," I acknowledged. It fosters a sense of community, and your dedication can earn you goodwill with colleagues and bosses. You are accessible and empathetic, and you are perceived as reliable.

"However, being too adherent can be misconstrued as a lack of ambition. This might lead to a loss of respect from those you hope to impress. Sacrificing your own voice to win approval can allow you to harbor resentment, helplessness, and perceived victimization that builds up over time.

"Think about it this way," I continued. "By constantly being agreeable, you set unhealthy boundaries. This can lead to frustration and a feeling of being unheard. Ultimately, it can even hinder your ability to fulfill your purpose, which I know is especially important to you and your faith journey."

Scott couldn't hold his head from nodding in agreement; it felt like he had an out-of-body experience.

On Monday evening, as Scott was getting ready to leave the office, he received a call from his friend, Sean, inviting him out for some food and drinks. When Sean asked where they should go, Scott, true to his compliant nature, replied, "Anywhere's fine, man!" But once they arrived at the bustling restaurant, with loud music filling the air and steaming hot dishes being brought to the table, Scott realized he would've much preferred a quieter spot with some Mexican food instead of the place his friend chose.

Reflecting on the evening, he later said to me, "It brought me right back to our last conversation, Jim, about my pattern of putting the needs of others ahead of mine. I could have just voiced my preference and probably enjoyed the evening a whole lot more."

Mike: Be Right or Be Gone

Mike's memories were the full opposite of the carefree Californian childhood depicted in movies. Born into a family that struggled to make ends meet, Mike's early years were marked by hardship and responsibility, which informed his definition of a strong leader. Being the eldest of four siblings, he was thrust into a role that demanded maturity far beyond his years. His family's financial constraints meant there were no toys, no birthday parties filled with presents, no vacations, and certainly no luxuries. Every necessity had to be earned, mostly through sheer grit, intellectual prowess, and a keen sense of "figuring it out." This is the reality that shaped Mike's character and future.

The lack of a strong parental support system further strengthened Mike's self-reliance. His father was a man of humble means and yet a skilled one. He was a mechanic by necessity rather than trade, always found in the garage with grease-stained hands. Although he never quite succeeded in his ventures, he instilled in Mike a crucial lesson: the value of hands-on work and the importance of learning. This was a lesson Mike took to heart. The garage became his extended classroom, a place where he learned to fix and repair not just machines but his perspective on life. When life seemed too complex, even as a child, Mike would retreat to the garage alone and emerge once he had figured out the "right" way to proceed, giving him a sense of calm—even if temporarily.

Mike's superior intellect was apparent early on. Despite the challenges at home, he excelled in school, quickly rising to the top of his class. His teachers recognized his potential and pushed him to apply for scholarships. Mike's academic brilliance earned him a full scholarship to a local prestigious private high school. This was not just a financial relief for his family but also a validation of his beliefs: he would rise from his current situation by receiving a superior education, amassing more knowledge, and earning respect and admiration along the way.

In high school, Mike stood out not just for his grades but for his ability to grasp complex concepts with ease. He became a tutor for his classmates, helping them with their studies. His friends' parents noticed his outstanding academic qualities and were grateful for his tutelage of their children. They would often invite him over for dinners, give him books and occasionally small gifts as tokens of appreciation. These gestures, though modest, were significant for

Mike. They reinforced the idea that his intellect was a valuable asset, one that could open doors and create opportunities.

Mike's responsibilities extended beyond academics. From a young age, he had to contribute to the family's finances. He took on odd jobs, from delivering newspapers to mowing lawns, and later found work at First Lead Technology Ltd. as a lab attendant. This job was more than just a source of income; it was an opportunity to learn and grow.

By the time Mike started working at First Lead Technology Ltd., his identity as the "problem solver" was firmly established. His colleagues, impressed by his ability to fix anything and everything, began seeking him out for solutions. He thrived in this role, reveling in the praise and the sense of control it brought.

Through these experiences, Mike developed a deep sense of self-reliance and an unshakable belief in his intellectual abilities. He understood that knowledge was power and that continuous learning was the key to success. This mindset propelled him through high school and into landing a full-time salaried position at First Lead Technology Ltd with only a high school diploma!

But now, many years later as a CEO, he sought out coaching. Mike had to admit his need for help. Here he was, burned out and confused. He'd always found safety in his ability to figure out the problem. He was perplexed he couldn't figure this one out. By solving the problems in the past, he'd been able to make things easier. But now as CEO, the problems didn't stop, and things seemed to get more complex with every decision he made. He was losing the same control he thought he earned through his vast repository of knowledge. This feeling didn't go away even at home; he didn't feel smart enough to know how to control his children's or his grandchildren's choices, nor did he have control of his time.

His strong intellect had brought him this far, making him CEO. But he was now feeling stuck. On his journey to the top, he overly relied on his intellect. But it was becoming apparent that he hadn't developed some of the other essential skills of executive leaders, such as empathy, trust, collaboration, and the ability to leverage the gifts of others.

"You have to let go of some of that control if you ever want to learn anything new, Mike," I said.

· CHAPTER THREE ·

SHIFTING FROM "OR" TO "AND"

Susan: Control AND Connection

Susan sat across from me, the summary of her completed leadership exercise laid out on the table. She had requested this meeting in person to go over the data from her 360 report again. It was one of those rare in-person meetings, and the atmosphere in the room was thick with anticipation. The assessment summary was eye-opening, yet it was the explanation that followed that really hit home for Susan. As she read through, it felt like she was being introduced to a stranger, yet somehow that stranger was also deeply familiar.

I began to explain, "A reactive leader is someone who's more focused on avoiding failure than on creating success." This was a concept that felt completely foreign to Susan, who had always viewed herself as a driven, ambitious businesswoman. This ambition was the source of success for her. She couldn't imagine how she was focused on avoiding failure.

Susan had often spoken of a longing for deeper relationships in her life, so I followed up with a question, "How does your need to be in control prevent you from building the relationships you desire?" Susan's expression tightened as she attempted to make the connection. I asked the question differently, "What is it you fear if you take your foot off the pedal propelling you towards success?"

"I guess I fear that people won't like me as much or that I won't be important to them," she replied. "Now that you've pointed it out, I only feel like I'm worthy of their respect if I'm successful."

"I didn't point that out, Susan. You did," I cut in immediately.

The realization dawned on her as she reflected on her answers to the questions. She could now see how her fear of being controlled, rather than the one in control had been her driving force. She feared that being under someone else's control could lead to the loss of her independence and an eventual dependency on someone else.

The previous relationships in her life came to mind: her dad, her college boyfriend, her ex-husband. In each relationship, she felt controlled and unable to assert her own ideas or opinions. Susan was surprised to realize that her need to control her businesses had little to do with the businesses themselves, but more to do with her desire not to lose her independence. This is how she realized she was protecting what she had gained, rather than creating what she wanted to have. The primary emotional energy behind most of her decisions was rooted in anxiety and inner conflict. If she wanted meaningful relationships more, the implication was clear. To be in a relationship with others meant there would have to be some dependency, placing her in a situation where she felt vulnerable. That was scary for her.

Susan was silent, absorbing the weight of this clarity. She had built her empire on a foundation of control and perfectionism, pillars of strength in her world. But now she was beginning to see that these pillars were also the source of her isolation and the strain on her relationships.

"How is your need to be seen as valuable or worthy connected with your relentless drive toward success and perfection?" I asked. Susan didn't say a word, but her eyes revealed the answers. She had always sought validation from the outside world—the applause of the crowd, the respect of her peers, and the approval of her dad. It was as if her self-worth was inextricably tied to the opinions of others.

"Where else in your life does this desire to be perfect and in control manifest?" I inquired. Susan began to reflect more on the patterns in her home, family, and relationships. She realized she had trapped herself in a never-ending cycle of proving her worth to others.

She reflected more deeply on her leadership approach: "I think I strive to take control because I appreciate it when people tell me that things are running like a well-oiled machine- smoothly and without any friction," she said. "When they don't, I start feeling inadequate or less than. To me, a leader is someone who always has everything under control, never letting anyone see them sweat."

"What do you tell yourself when things aren't running smoothly and others notice?" I asked.

"I often tell myself I'm not good enough, or I should have prevented that from happening in the first place," she sheepishly admitted.

"It's time you stopped "should-ing" every responsibility on yourself. You can't thrive under a cloud of shame," I warned her.

> **You can't thrive under a cloud of shame.**

She had always viewed the world as a competitive arena, where only the strongest survived. This mindset had served her well in business, propelling her to success, but it had also created a chasm in her personal life. Her children felt smothered, her friends undervalued, and her employees that they had no room to innovate or expand on her ideas. While people said Susan was generally a nice person and they didn't dislike her, few could say they actually knew her, and some even said they felt like she was hiding a part of her.

"When I interact with you, I see that you've built your sense of self around your ability to control lots of variables at once. Your quest for perfection drives you to seek improvements, and you excel in many situations. You set incredibly high standards for yourself, often unattainable ones. You influence others too. You always take responsibility and get straight to action."

Susan nodded, recognizing these traits in herself. She was indeed a visionary, a problem-solver, and a leader. But now she began to see the shadow these strengths cast.

Susan reflected on her observations. "It's like seeing how my dad led, and I have tried to take the good parts and avoid the bad parts. I want to be seen as nice and friendly. But instead of honoring the gifts of the controlling nature, I suppress them. I desire to be in connected and authentic relationships more than anything. But I seem unable to take my hands off the helm most of the time, "she said to herself. "How do I maintain my sense of control and have healthy, connected relationships?"

Susan continued to reflect. She realized that her singular focus on her success had caused her to overlook the needs of those around her. She had sacrificed relationships in pursuit of achieving results. "I've tried to not be controlling by trying to be intentionally generous. But then people seem to feel I'm being manipulative or that there are strings attached to my generosity. I feel like I can't win. As I say it out loud, I sound like a horrible person," she said, trying hard not to look straight into my eyes.

"No, Susan, it makes you sound like a person who has just gained enormous insight that you can use for change," I offered a reframe.

"I am tired of reacting to what I might lose. I want to lean into what I have to gain. I have a lot to learn," Susan explained with a steely resolve that was coming through more abundantly and authentically.

"Exactly," I responded. "You are ready to learn about creating your future rather than just reacting to the circumstances. It requires becoming more self-aware, taking the time to reflect, and learning to lead from within. We need to embrace the strengths and the shadows. To become aware allows us the capacity to harness the energy. It's about creating powerfully, not just controlling outcomes."

For Susan, the idea of creating her future with a full view of what she wanted was new, something she had never consciously done. She now saw that she had operated with a mindset to survive, maintaining her sense of being in control—but at the expense of her connections. She was so focused on not losing what she had built and striving to have more as a means to prove her value. But now, she saw a different kind of victory on the horizon. It wasn't just about external achievements anymore; it was about finding fulfillment, purpose, and meaning in her life. She could create a future with both control AND connection.

As Susan left the session, she felt a renewed sense of purpose. The road ahead was daunting; it would require her to unlearn a lifetime of conditioning and to rewire her brain to embrace this new "and" mindset. But as she walked out into the sunlight, she knew that she was ready. She could see a different path, one that was both fulfilling and empowering, waiting for her to take the first step.

Scott: Boldness AND Belonging

As the coaching session drew to a close, I observed that Scott Ford felt a mix of relief and unease. On one hand, the insights he had gained were liberating; it was as if a veil had been lifted. On the other hand, the realization of his long-standing patterns was unsettling.

As we reviewed the insights he gained from the leadership exercise, I asked, "How does aligning with other people's opinions give you a feeling of safety and security?"

Scott paused, then replied, "I feel like I belong more, that I'm accepted, or that I know that I'm doing a good job when I accomplish what they want me to."

I followed up, "How is that behavior also frustrating you?"

He swallowed hard before admitting, "I've spent most of my life bending to the will of others. Essentially, I've made them happy but lost myself in the process."

"What is it that you fear if you assert your own opinion?" I asked, hoping to elicit some insight.

"I fear someone will tell me I'm wrong, or laugh at me. Or think that I'm incompetent."

"And if they do, what would you feel?" I probed further.

"That they don't value me or that I'm no longer needed."

"So, it sounds like it's really your fear of being ostracized or rejected that drives you to compliance," I reflected. "It's almost as if you've internalized a belief system that reinforces this behavior."

We continued with a short exercise.

"Fill in the blank with me: "*I'm _____ when I'm liked.*"

"Valued," Scott responded.

"*I'm _____ when I'm agreeable.*"

"Safe," Scott replied.

"*When I meet others' expectations, I am _____.*"

"Successful," said Scott.

Scott's expression brightened as he realized new insights from the leadership exercise. He had mostly been navigating the world with this internal script, a silent dialogue that prioritized harmony and peace above all else. He would often mistake dissent from others or himself, as a sign of his unworthiness to belong. He had become an expert at saying "yes" when he meant "no" to maintain the façade of agreement to prevent discord.

"This nature has its strengths," I said. "You're empathetic, loyal, and reliable. You're a team player who consistently goes the extra mile." I then asked, "What are the downsides to this nature?"

Scott took some time before answering, "I have a constant need to please, to belong, to be liked. I sometimes feel helpless, and I end up sacrificing my desires and goals for the sake of others."

Scott had often felt like a passive observer in his own life, more reactive than proactive. His ambition, though present, had been overshadowed by his desire to maintain the status quo and keep everyone around him happy.

> **Leadership is going places you've never been before and taking people along the journey with you.**

"In leadership, this compliance can be particularly limiting," I told him, my tone firm but understanding. "Leadership is going places you've never been before and taking people along the journey with you. Especially executive leadership, which you're now expected to exhibit as CFO."

Hoping to help with more connections, I asked rhetorically, "How does prioritizing the need to belong and for harmony get in the way of innovation and growth?"

Scott had always believed that his leadership style was based on consensus and collaboration. But now, he was beginning to see that he had often sacrificed his own ideals for the sake of unity. Instead of being a visionary leader, he had become more of a facilitator, smoothing over conflicts rather than driving change.

"To truly lead, you need to move beyond compliance and embrace your inner authority," I advised. "This means developing a clear vision for yourself and your organization and being willing to make tough decisions, even if they aren't popular." Scott had always been so focused on following the rules and meeting expectations that he hadn't really considered the possibility of a different future—one where he defined the rules and set the expectations. His fear of failure had kept him from taking risks, from making bold decisions that could have led to greater success and personal fulfillment. "But you need to realize executive leaders are expected to self-author—to bring their vision to reality and to drive systemic changes—all things that are sure to ruffle a few feathers of both executives and

> **Most people want what change will bring. Few actually want to change.**

subordinates. Most people want what change will bring. Few actually want to change."

Scott was beginning to see just how his past was influencing his present. He didn't have to choose between being bold or belonging. Rather, he had to figure out how to inextricably link both together in his own way. Breaking free from a lifetime of conditioning would be no easy task. It would require courage, determination, and a willingness to embrace discomfort. But the first step was already taken— awareness.

Scott's journey to authenticity would be challenging, filled with obstacles both internal and external. But something inside of him had shifted; and though his mind was ready to consider the possibility of changing, his heart was still undecided.

As he got ready to log off our virtual session, I could see Scott pondering the choices before him. He could continue to exist as a man burdened by the expectations of others or become a leader ready to carve out a future that was truly his own, fostering growth and transformation.

Mike: Intellect AND Inclusion

Mike Flair had long built his career and sense of self-worth on the belief that his superior intellect was his greatest asset. From an early age, he found comfort in being the smartest person in the room. This intellect was more than just a tool for success; it was his armor against a world that often felt uncertain and threatening. For Mike, being right wasn't just a habit; it was his refuge. This mindset, which had propelled him to remarkable achievements, also created a barrier between him and those around him.

As Mike climbed the corporate ladder to become the CEO of First Lead Technology Ltd., he leaned more heavily on what he perceived earned him the CEO title: his intellect. He was convinced that his sharp mind and unique insights were the key drivers of the company's success and ultimately his sense of security. "A leader has to have the right answers, or they are not fit to be so," he told me in our first session. As a result, he often felt that he alone had to solve the company's problems, shouldering the burden of leadership almost entirely on his own. If the company failed, Mike feared he would certainly return to the humble beginnings of his childhood, which he had worked so hard to get away from.

Mike's intellectual prowess brought undeniable benefits. He had a rare ability to cut through the complexities that others missed, offering unique perspectives that were often both insightful and valuable. He cared deeply about those close to him and was passionately committed to causes he believed in. His solution-oriented mindset often led to wise decisions, and his drive for excellence pushed him and his company to new heights. Yet, as he moved into this role as CEO, these strengths that had propelled him now seemed to be holding him back from achieving his greatest leadership accomplishments.

Mike's need to find the right answer gave him an air of superiority and prevented him from seeing other people's viewpoints. In meetings, he admitted to often finding himself tuning out, confident that he already knew the best course of action. When his nerves were shot, he would even label others' ideas or solutions as "stupid," something he would regret but continue to do. This attitude stifled collaboration and innovation, as his team members felt their input was neither needed nor valued. Over time, his behavior eroded trust and was slowly creating a culture of disengagement. His leadership team often silently wondered if they were in the right position or how long they could put up with his type of leadership. His constant need to bolster his self-esteem by proving his ideas correct rather than seeking wisdom from others led to burnout and dissatisfaction, eventually prompting him to seek coaching at Conjunction Leadership.

During our sessions, I guided Mike to reflect on something he had never fully considered: his over-reliance on intellect as a means of self-protection. "Mike," I offered, after listening to him describe his struggles, "leadership requires a strong ego, but when that ego becomes over-inflated, it can create problems. A leader who demands too much attention for themselves fails to build a strong team, and as a result, the full potential of the people around them often goes untapped.

"I want you to consider how your need to be 'right' prevents you from hearing others." I let the statement linger in the air.

Mike began to understand that his need to be right and to maintain a sense of superiority was preventing him from becoming the empowering leader he wanted to be. Just as importantly, he realized that having grown up learning every aspect of the business, he believed he knew everything there was to know. His identity was deeply tied to this knowledge. Less consciously, he viewed others as not having much knowledge or simply not knowing enough, which led him to feel a moral obligation to share what he knew. Without realizing it, he became known as a "know-it-all" to those around him. This caused others to hold back from sharing their opinions or asking questions, out of fear of "being wrong" or, worse, "being seen as incompetent." As a result, Mike felt he had to carry the burden of all the decision-making, believing those around him simply weren't capable.

This realization marked a turning point for Mike. He recognized that to be an effective leader, he needed to disrupt these deeply ingrained behaviors. His intellect had been helpful so far, and now he needed to put it to use again by developing new behaviors of including others in his thought process so they could assume more leadership roles in the company and give him the much-needed gift of rest.

"I want the whole team to 'get it right' and do it together. I'm tired of doing it all alone. I guess you could say I want intellect AND inclusion." This was the clearest statement of intent I had heard him utter thus far.

Over the next several months, I guided Mike through a process of self-awareness and growth. The first step was to recognize and accept his need for superiority and how it was affecting his relationships and leadership roles. This would not be an easy task for the self-avowed "smartest person in the room." But Mike was determined to bridge this gap.

Mike realized he could draw on his uncanny ability to learn quickly. But instead of learning the technical aspects of the business, he set out to learn what he'd always considered as "soft." But now, he was realizing those skills were actually quite "hard" to acquire.

Mike knew he had to start listening actively and attuning to emotions—his and others. Instead of mentally preparing his responses or solutions while others were speaking, Mike focused on fully engaging with and understanding their perspectives. As he began to genuinely consider the ideas and insights of his team, he discovered the value of diverse viewpoints. He saw that when people felt heard and valued, their contributions became more meaningful and often led to innovative solutions.

Mike also realized that empowering his team to take ownership of their projects not only lightened his workload, it fostered a sense of trust and collaboration as well. By stepping back and allowing others to lead, he created an environment where his team could thrive and develop their problem-solving skills.

Another critical aspect of Mike's growth was embracing vulnerability. Acknowledging that he didn't have all the answers and that it was okay to seek help represented a significant shift in his mindset. This vulnerability made him more approachable and relatable, which in turn helped to build stronger, more authentic relationships with his team and family. Simply asking, "What other perspectives am I missing?" was a huge step for Mike in his daily interactions with others. Learning to actually listen—while reserving judgment on their response—took his leadership to a whole new level.

He learned to balance his usual directive style with a supportive stance. He started focusing on developing the capabilities of his team members, helping them grow and succeed. This change not only improved the overall performance of the company but also reduced Mike's burnout and stress. He found that by trusting his team and valuing their input, he could focus on the strategic aspects of his role, leading the company with a broader, more visionary perspective.

At home, Mike's reformed approach had a positive impact as well. He began to apply the same principles of active listening and vulnerability with his wife, Lily, and their children. Instead of trying to control or judge their decisions, he offered support and guidance. This change helped to rebuild trust and strengthen his relationships with his family.

As Mike continued to grow in his leadership role, he came to understand that his true identity wasn't just about being the person with the most superior knowledge. It was about being a leader who could inspire, support, and empower others. He learned that creating his ideal future meant creating an environment where everyone could succeed, not just him. By shifting his focus from being right to being inclusive and helping other people develop their own self-reliance, Mike discovered a deeper sense of fulfillment and purpose.

He moved from a place of intellectual superiority to a position of authentic leadership. His willingness to confront and disrupt his patterns of behavior led to a more inclusive, collaborative, and empowered organization. Not to mention, he started to feel excitement and relief return to his daily life.

· CHAPTER FOUR ·

ALIGNING NEEDS AND VALUES

S usan arrived early for her session, her face a blend of resolve and unease. She had been reflecting deeply on what it meant to be a better leader. "I've realized that before I can be a better leader," she confessed to me, "I must first become a better human being."

"That's great," I said, "But how do you intend to achieve that?"

"I've mastered the art of task management and control—maybe even too much," she replied. "But I have a lot to learn about relating to others authentically, building relationships over our shared experiences without the need to sacrifice my own voice for the sake of maintaining control."

> **Before I become a better leader, I must first become a better human being.**

Her honesty was refreshing, and I smiled, knowing she was on the right path. We exchanged a few more pleasantries before she hesitated, then posed a question that had clearly been weighing on her mind. "Jim," she began slowly, "I need your help with something that's been affecting another relationship—my relationship with my husband."

She went on to explain, her voice laced with concern. "My husband, James, has raised some issues about my continued absence at home. To be honest, he's been very understanding, but he says that while he understands my work schedule, I tend to work even when I'm home—taking calls and responding to emails when I should be spending time with him and the kids."

Susan, a driven entrepreneur with multiple businesses under her belt, manages to juggle an impressive workload. Each of her companies has its own president, yet she maintains close oversight, insisting on daily reports and being heavily involved in decision-making. However, this level of involvement had begun to strain her relationship with James and their children.

James had expressed his concerns in no uncertain terms. "The kids need you. I need you. We want you to be present," he had told her one night as she wound down from yet another long day. The look of stress on her face as she disclosed this to me was impossible to miss.

"Susan," I said gently, "this might be a good time to talk about needs and values."

She looked at me quizzically. "Needs and values?" she repeated, trying to decipher the connection to her situation.

"Yes," I nodded. "They are crucial in understanding how we show up in our everyday lives and the decisions we make. Your needs and values are like the compass and map guiding you through life's terrain."

Susan adjusted herself in her seat, her curiosity piqued. She was beginning to see where this conversation was heading.

"Values," I began, "are how we derive our sense of worth, meaning, and purpose from life. They are often rooted in morality or spirituality, and they guide us in our interactions with others. As we advance in life and career, we choose certain values to live by—whether it's integrity, leadership, relationships, or family. These values are what we spend most of our energy on."

Susan nodded as she took notes, clearly curious.

"But needs," I continued, "are different. Needs are something we don't choose. They drive how we unconsciously or less consciously respond to the world around us. Needs are often driven by our experiences and the way our brains have been wired to seek safety. We can be aware of them sometimes. Needs come before values. Always."

I paused, giving her a moment to absorb the distinction. "Most people don't like to admit they have needs because it can make them feel vulnerable, dependent, or needy." I could see her shift in her chair, a sign that this may be too close to home for her. "But we all have them. Needs can be as basic as the need for connection and love or more complex, like the need for freedom, the need to be heard, or the need for affirmation."

I observed Susan reflecting deeply, likely considering how her own needs had been shaped by her upbringing. She had often spoken of her strict, controlling father, who demanded obedience and only seemed pleased when she completed her chores or was engaged in productive activities like studying instead of watching television. These early experiences undoubtedly influenced her strong drive to work hard and achieve.

"So, do our needs always align with our values?" she asked.

"Good question," I replied. "At different points in our lives, we all struggle to align our needs with our values. In fact, sometimes we violate our values to meet a pressing need."

I gave her an example to illustrate. "I had a client once with a strong need for appreciation and affirmation. They identified one of their core values was honesty. Yet, they found themselves telling half-truths and lying to their boss and colleagues just to get a 'great job' or a nod of approval. They were compromising their values. From an objective point of view, we can see that they placed an immediate need above their deeper value, satisfying that need quickly but at the expense of who they truly wanted to be. It's exhausting living outside of your values."

Another example came to mind, one that resonated with Susan's current situation. "Consider someone who has a need to be in control and a value to create belonging for themselves and others," I continued. Susan knew immediately we were describing her present dilemma. "This person may find that they choose to work extra hard, stay at the office late, or attend an urgent meeting at the expense of going home and engaging in nurturing their closest relationships.

"One is a need. The other appears to be a want. It's almost as if the hunger of the need will get met even at the expense of something more fulfilling, such as the value of being cared for and caring for others in a relationship."

"Hmmm... Hmmm... Very true, Jim," Susan said, her voice tinged with recognition.

I leaned forward, wanting to drive the point home. When we don't live according to our chosen values, we may not be judged by others, but we feel it within ourselves. There's an internal tension that drains us because, deep down, we know we've made choices that don't align with the person we intend to be or our true self.

"This tension," I explained, "is a struggle between safety and purpose. Our brains are hardwired to prioritize safety—to scratch that itch or get that quick fix. But when we consistently choose to live by our values, we find a deeper sense of control and direction in our lives. We begin to feel that our choices and actions are right, not just for us, but in a broader sense of what is good and just."

> **Our brains are hardwired to prioritize safety.**

I shared a personal story to illustrate how this dynamic had played out in my own life.

Growing up, my father was strict, demanding productivity and detesting idleness. Saturdays and holidays were reserved for chores, and anything less than full engagement in work attracted his ire. My brain quickly adapted to receiving the approval that came when I completed my chores and likewise the criticism that came when I was caught being "lazy." I became conditioned to seek fulfillment through productivity. For years, I found satisfaction in being busy, in achieving, and in ticking off tasks.

But as I grew older and moved out of the house, I realized that productivity, which led to constant busyness, had me burned out and on anxiety's doorstep. I knew I was busy, but I didn't feel I was truly productive. I kept busy with learning my job. Furthering my career. Getting good results for my employer. At the same time, I felt a misalignment with my values of mentoring and being present with my children. I didn't understand this for a long time. I assumed they would grant me favor because, after all, I was providing for their basic needs. However, at the end of my corporate career, I decided to redefine what "productivity" meant to me. And I had to create my own definition of success, which included more significance and less success. This allowed me to embrace values that would ground me and bring me peace, even if it meant setting boundaries that sometimes felt uncomfortable. Because I had a greater sense of control over how I invested my time, I chose how to schedule work and client interactions around the opportunities to invest in my children. And to be honest, I would start to feel way more fulfilled as a person, leader, and father.

"In aligning my needs with my values," I told Susan, "I learned to protect my values by establishing boundaries and standards. It's not always easy, but it's essential for leading a life that feels true and fulfilling."

Susan listened intently while reflecting. "It seems my need for control and my need for belonging are in conflict. On one hand, I fear that if I exert my need for control, I will be unlikable or even perceived by others as "bitchy," which is one word I fear the most. So, I am wrestling with how to honor my need to control without ruining my relationship with the people I want to be around and work with."

I asked, "How might you communicate what you expect and the standards of performance you want to see while also focusing on the relationship you desire to preserve?"

Susan remarked, "I guess I need to be more clear up front so I'm not as passive-aggressive later on. I need to just tell people what I'm thinking rather than ask them what they are thinking first and hope it aligns with my thoughts."

She paused for a moment and then asked, "But how do we reach this point of self-awareness where we can align our needs with our values?"

"Leadership is a journey. Not a destination," I responded. "It's not something you arrive at overnight. Some people start this journey early, while others begin later in life. Experiences—especially those that challenge us—can lead to greater self-awareness. But it's a continuous process. Needs scream loudly—like a hungry toddler in a grocery store! It's our job as the parent of ourselves to learn how to meet their hunger without turning them into tyrants who misbehave to get whatever they want."

> **Leadership is a journey. Not a destination.**

Susan nodded, her mind already working through how she could apply this to her own life. "I understand," she said thoughtfully. "It's about making conscious choices and being aware of what is truly important to us."

"Exactly," I agreed. "And with this awareness, you can start to make decisions that align your actions with your values, rather than just reacting to immediate needs."

I then suggested an exercise that might help her clarify her own needs and values. "Would you be interested in completing a worksheet that can help you dig deeper into this?" I asked.

"Yeah, I think that would be helpful," she replied.

I explained the intricacies of the worksheet and promised to email it to her after our session. As we wrapped up, Susan seemed more resolved. "I'll consider this progress," she said with a smile.

I chuckled and added, "Remember, knowledge is progress, Susan, but wisdom is our end goal."

Before we ended our session, I asked her what her next steps would be. Susan was clear. She would talk to James, share what she had learned, and work on establishing boundaries that would allow her to create a greater sense of belonging with her family while still managing her businesses effectively.

We scheduled our next appointment, and Susan clicked off the call.

Two days after our session, Susan texted me to share an insight she had gained about her need for control reflecting on her everyday life. She recalled an angry client asking for an immediate meeting to resolve a difficult situation. Feeling the pressure to regain control, she nearly conceded to the after-hours teleconference. She knew she'd already promised James a quiet night at home, and she knew this meeting would jeopardize that sense of belonging and the relationship she coveted with her husband. "I recalled the hungry toddler, and man was he screaming," the words in bold. "I thought of needs and values and how to align them."

"And what did you do?" I asked.

"At that moment I knew what I needed to do. I told the client I could happily meet with them tomorrow afternoon and we'd take care of their situation at once. Then I drove home peacefully in my car to James and the kids. It was liberating and didn't feel rude or "bitchy" as I feared. James was happy. The client was happy. And most importantly, I was happy. Boundaries do work!"

· CHAPTER FIVE ·

THE LEADERSHIP MIRROR

Susan started our next conversation by reviewing her progress, aligning needs and values. "I think I know why Paul left," she blurted. "My frustration was never about him. It was about me."

"Interesting," I said. "Care to elaborate?"

"I never wanted Paul to feel controlled. He was the original founder and a brilliant guy in his own right," she began.

Yet, Susan felt out of control when around him, and many of his actions she perceived as disorganized. In such times, she took it as a judgment of her ability to maintain control. So instead of telling him what she wanted—or better yet, needed, as she'd learned from her need to be in control—she made suggestions. And lots of them. She suggested weekly reports detailing his every action and decision. She suggested he use the new software to track his projects. And yet, he never implemented these suggestions. All of this effort left Susan feeling disrespected and drained.

"In a sense I was trying to get him to commit to actions that would give *me* a sense of control. But that wasn't his need," she continued. "It was mine. Now I see he took those for what they were—suggestions. If I could do it differently, I would have brought my value for belonging up and coupled it closely with my need for control."

In Susan's account of how things played out, she could have simply told him her need and how she would like to get that need met and been more direct with her expectations. Then she could have facilitated a conversation around how to help get his and her needs met, which would have brought them both closer to belonging. It would have been more direct, kinder, simpler, and helped them both get what they wanted.

"I think he left because he felt controlled as if there was something wrong with him because he wasn't like me." Susan confessed. "I wish I would have seen this earlier."

"That's quite an insight, Susan. It's what I call the leadership mirror," I said. "You can spend a lot of needless energy trying to get people to change, but what frustrates you about them is often something that you're frustrated with in yourself. It doesn't matter when you learn this, but that you do learn it while you can still do something with it. 'If you're not dead, you're not done,' you often have to remind yourself.

> **If you're not dead, you're not done.**

"Are you ready to dive in and learn the secret to preserving your energy?" I asked.

"Of course. I can always use more energy!" she said enthusiastically.

"The secret is boundaries," I explained. "Understanding your needs and values gives you a clear set of boundaries—lines you draw in the sand regarding what you're willing to do and what you're not. These boundaries aren't just protective barriers; they're vital guidelines for how you govern your life, ensuring that your actions are in alignment with the person you aspire to be."

Susan reflected on this.

"To live in alignment, it's crucial to protect your values and needs, especially when circumstances tempt you to compromise them," I continued, drawing upon her reflections with Paul. "Now that you've had this insight, you'll be less likely to suggest actions in the future—or at least you'll be more likely to be explicit about the difference between a directive and a suggestion.

"This is now a boundary, and by asserting it, you protect yourself from wasting energy feeling disrespected and trying to change the other party to regain your sense of control. You'll be more direct in stating your needs. You will clearly know what to do and what not to do in similar situations. And the important thing is, you'll waste less energy!"

"That makes so much sense," Susan replied thoughtfully.

"It's similar to lying or telling half-truths just to gain approval from your boss or subordinate," I continued. "If truth and honesty are values you hold dear, every time you distort the truth, you're eroding those values and simultaneously eroding your precious energy as you draw dissonance between who you think you are and how you're behaving. Establishing boundaries helps you protect what matters most to you. It ensures that your actions are in alignment with your values, making you congruent with the person you want to be."

Susan was scribbling furiously, taking notes but also reflecting deeply on our conversation. I could tell that she was processing not just the information but also its implications for her own life and leadership.

"When you set strong boundaries," I explained, "you naturally create high standards. These standards aren't just about what you expect of yourself. They can also create an implicit understanding of what you expect from others. They define what you will and will not tolerate in your interactions and decisions. Here's where you have to be careful. You can't expect everyone else to have the same standards as you have, lest you become critical of their efforts."

"I'm thinking about the times when I didn't have strong boundaries," Susan said. "When my needs got met but I knew I was living outside my values. I knew something was wrong, and I was constantly second-guessing myself."

"That's called judgment," I said. "You were judging yourself against the values of how you saw yourself.

"And when you live in judgment, you exhaust precious mental resources. You experience more shame, anxiety, and regret. Because you don't like to feel those things, it's easier to start looking outward. You expect others to live to your standards and you start judging them and seeing their faults—in essence, to take the pressure off of you and focus your energy on something or someone else."

Susan looked up from her notes, her eyes meeting mine with a mixture of curiosity and understanding. "Are you saying this is why I was growing frustrated with Paul?"

"Exactly," I said. "Your standards give you a benchmark for what you consider acceptable. The things that bother you about other people often reflect something inside you that you are aware of but unwilling to change. In other words, as you judge others, you are running away from your ability to judge yourself appropriately and hold yourself to your own standards."

Susan had now begun to translate this insight to her situation to test what she was learning. She didn't have a very good alignment of her needs and values. And this led to her trying to exert control over Paul so she could feel better about feeling out of control. This led to their relationship eroding. She felt disrespected, he felt micromanaged, and neither of them felt like they belonged in the relationship. Then, because she was living in judgment over herself and not meeting her own standards for being more in control, she further focused her attention on Paul, expecting him to live up to the same standards she would have for herself in an "out of control" situation.

"Boy! This is complicated. No wonder I'm exhausted most of the time," Susan exclaimed

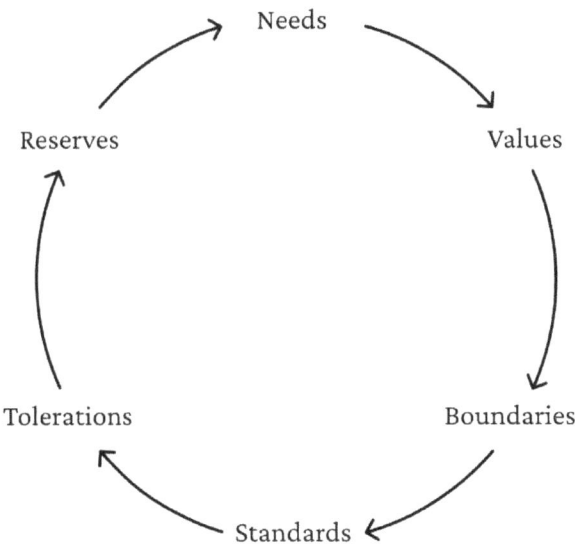

"Exactly, Susan," I said. "If your boundaries are too weak, your standards will be low and judgement will be high. You'll be more critical of yourself and of the situation around you. And you feel exhausted all the time. Then you might find yourself tolerating mediocrity from your employees, feeling like you just don't have the energy to fight this battle. Or, conversely, you might find yourself overworking without complaint to try to regain a sense of control. Either way, a growing sense of resentment might set in. This depletes your reserves—your energy, your patience, your emotional well-being. And when your reserves are low, you become less aware of your needs and values, and the cycle continues."

"Now you're getting personal," she said jokingly. "I now see why I pick up the 'extra' work and simultaneously decide that people around me are just lazy. I don't have strong boundaries about speaking my truth and helping them grow through their mistakes because I didn't want to be seen as 'bossy.' I got more work, more frustration, and they got off Scott-free while I lived in judgment of myself and them."

I could see that the dots were connecting in Susan's mind. The cycle of misalignment I was describing was something she had lived through, something she was eager to break free from.

"It's a vicious cycle," I continued, my voice soft. "It all starts with understanding your needs. Do you know what they are? Do you know your values? Have you established strong boundaries to protect them? Do you have high standards that guide your actions? Are you living congruently with the person you want to be so that you stop condemning others? When you answer these questions, you can begin to stop tolerating the things that drain your energy. Your reserves will replenish, and you'll feel more grounded, more in alignment with who you are and who you say you want to be."

Susan tapped her foot on the floor, a subtle gesture that revealed just how much the conversation resonated with her.

"So, you're telling me the key to more energy is not more coffee?" she joked. "Seriously, this is brilliant and insightful," she said, sounding both relieved and aware.

And then, as if to make sure I heard her again, she summarized her learning. "Instead of trying to change Paul, I should have focused on changing myself."

"Yes, Susan. That is exactly the leadership mirror," I confirmed.

Susan realized that much of the burnout and frustration she had been experiencing with her subordinates stemmed from her own shortcomings as a leader. She had always attended conferences and read books on becoming a better leader. But she had been a passive reader, rather than an active participant. She failed to take action, to apply all she had learned from books and seminars towards her growth as a leader. "This is the crux of our discussion," Susan said, brimming with newfound conviction.

I smiled, knowing that she was beginning to see the profound impact that was linked between boundaries and energy reserves—and how it could transform her life and career.

"When you know your needs and values," I affirmed, "you can conduct your energy audit as you reflect at the end of each day and ask yourself, 'Did I live in alignment with my values today? Did I honor my boundaries?' If the answer is no, you'll feel it—you'll know that something is off, that you're not fully in alignment with the person you claim to be. And you'll know that by becoming a student of your energy - or a feeling of being "unstuck" in forward motion toward your ambitions."

"But how do we avoid falling into this trap?" Susan asked. "How do we prevent ourselves from slipping into misalignment, especially when it's so easy to get caught up in the demands of life?"

I didn't respond immediately, allowing Susan to reflect on her statement. "Our brains get wired for certain behaviors—they are designed to seek safety and avoid discomfort. But we are not just creatures of instinct; we are also beings with the capacity for purpose and meaning. This is where the spiritual aspect comes in. To truly live in alignment, we must go beyond our basic instincts and background experiences and tap into our higher selves, the part of us that seeks fulfillment, not just survival."

Susan listened intently, her face reflecting the seriousness of the moment. "So, it's about fighting that inner tension, the part of us that just wants to stay safe and comfortable?"

"Exactly," I said. "It's about recognizing that while your brain might push you toward the path of least resistance, your spirit is guiding you toward growth, purpose, and alignment. It's about making choices that reflect who you truly are, not just what feels safe in the moment. In a sense it's about learning how to stop reacting to the world around you and start creating the life you choose to live."

To illustrate this, I shared a personal example. I value my family deeply and desperately want to spend as much time with my kids as I can. Recently, my older kids were returning from college. This afforded us the rare opportunity for the entire family—all seven of us—to be together. But as more kids come home, so does more stuff. And after a stressful day working with clients, I entered our laundry room only to be greeted by piles and piles of dirty clothes. Immediately, my sense of shame—followed by disgust—kicked in. 'I should have anticipated there to be more laundry. Why couldn't they wash their own clothes? No one even appreciates how much I support this family.' The voices in my head were screaming. Clearly my brain was hijacked. So, what did I do? I focused on doing the laundry, begrudgingly. It was completely out of character and alignment with the quality time I wanted to be spending which was compounding my anger and frustration. Fortunately, I caught myself.

My brain was wired to focus on productivity to earn my sense of relationship and doing the laundry seemed like it would get me the relationship approval I was desperately wanting. But I had to override my ingrained pattern of earning my approval through productivity. I had to define that my biggest need was approval and bringing that into alignment with my value of family meant I needed to invest time with them right now—even if the laundry was piled high. And by living into my values, I was able to regain a sense of composure and replenish my reserves. That day I decided to measure my productivity in the number of moments I created with my kids, not the amount of laundry I washed.

"That's a powerful example, Jim," Susan said smiling after I concluded my story. "It reminds me that time is finite, and we're not guaranteed endless opportunities to live purposefully. We need to start prioritizing what truly matters."

I nodded, appreciating her insight. "Exactly. When you live in alignment with your values and needs, you become the best version of yourself. And when you model that behavior, others will follow. They'll see that you're not just talking the talk—you're walking the walk."

Susan sat back in her chair. "This is incredibly motivating and helpful," she said, a sense of calm settling over her. "Thank you, Jim. I feel like I finally understand how to move forward."

"You're welcome, Susan," I replied, smiling warmly. "Remember, this journey is ongoing but it always starts from within. If you're starting with someone else, you're starting in the wrong direction. As you continue to establish and honor your boundaries, you'll find that living in alignment becomes almost second nature. And when that happens, you'll not only feel more fulfilled, but you'll also inspire others to do the same."

Before she left, I had one final question: "What will you do with what we've talked about today?"

"I'm going to start conducting regular energy audits, reflecting on where I've let my energy drain and how to better protect it to be congruent with the person I am aspiring to be. This will help me build the relationships I want while being in control of myself and my life."

> **This journey is ongoing but it always starts from within.**

As our session came to a close, I could see the transformation in Susan. She was no longer the frazzled, overburdened leader who had called me up a few months ago. She was becoming someone who understood the power of boundaries, someone who was ready to live in alignment with her true self.

And that, I knew, was the key to her long-term success and happiness.

· CHAPTER SIX ·

LEARNING TO "BE" INSTEAD OF "DO"

Susan showed up on my screen, her energy noticeably different from previous sessions. She smiled, but it was the smile of someone navigating a season of deep reflection, perhaps even an inner struggle. After a few moments of catching up, she began sharing her thoughts from the past weekend—a time she had spent with her kids.

"We had a little family time before the craziness of high school kicked in for them," she said. "They're growing so fast. I feel like the house is gradually emptying."

The reality of children growing up, moving on, and the quiet that follows is a season many parents wrestle with. The shift from full, bustling households to quieter, more reflective homes is inevitable, but it's not always easy to accept. I could sense that Susan was grappling with this transition, not just in her family life but in other areas of her world as well.

"So, where are we heading today?" I asked, smiling, trying to lighten the mood as I sensed her thoughts lingering in that space.

Susan glanced at me, a sarcastic smile playing on her lips. "I can't say exactly," she admitted with a casual shrug. "But that 'being versus doing' concept has been on my mind. I'm constantly meditating on it."

I nodded. We'd spoken about this before. Susan had begun applying all her newfound insights and it helped her redistribute her workload. A key to this accomplishment was her energy audits and corresponding better boundaries—she more vigorously protected her time, especially time she considered sacred to maintain her emotional reserves. She had made the conscious choice to stop taking calls during weekends and was allowing the presidents of each of her businesses to step up and take charge more often, holding them accountable for doing so and offering guidance instead of taking over whenever she sensed things were about to get out of control.

Yet she was a person caught up in the personal growth space of having to consistently "do" things to get better.

"You keep saying that we are human beings, not human doings. But I'm still not sure I know how to apply that," she stated almost in the form of a question. "I want to be a better wife, mother and overall person, but I'm still not sure what I need to do to become that."

It was a moment of clarity, an admission that her focus was beginning to shift away from the hustle and achievements that had consumed so much of her attention. But I needed her to dig deeper. "What gets in the way of you being a great wife and mother, Susan?" I prompted.

> **We are human beings, not human doings.**

"I get so focused on what I'm doing and what I need to do that I often miss where I am and who I'm with," she admitted. "I want to stop missing things—you know the really important things—for the sake of the busyness and trivial things. I guess I want to be more present."

I could sense she was in a deep place of reflection so I dug even further to see what meaning she could attach to her intent, "If you were more present in all of your interactions, then what would you have?" I probed.

Susan was silent for a moment. Then, she said, "I get so focused on doing. Then when I do things, I sort of expect someone will notice and tell me, 'Good job.' When I hear that, then I get a sense that I am valued, which may be a cheap alternative for my need to belong."

"So, belonging—that's what you would have if you were more present. Amazing!" I said summarily. "Let me lead you on a journey through some questions.

"What keeps you from being present?"

"I worry about keeping up. I get anxious that things are going to get out of control. I start thinking if I take time away that the work will be worse later when I come back to it. It just piles up, you know. I feel like I just have to keep shoveling or I'll get buried alive."

"And how is that affecting your reserves?"

"It drains them. A lot. There's not enough coffee in the world to keep me going some days."

"And how does having your reserves drained affect your ability to be present?" I asked her.

"When I'm tired or spent, I'm certainly not at my best and am very edgy," Susan admitted. "And when I try to push through, it just gets worse from there. It's a dangerous spiral. The more I push on the more I deplete my reserves and the more I just try to keep pushing."

"However, when you are more present and attuned to the conversations with your family and loved ones and ultimately create a greater sense of belonging for you and for them, how would that affect your reserves?" I asked further.

Susan leaned forward, "They would be increased! I love those moments. Even though the conversation is difficult, I walk away feeling like I just hit a home run. I'm tired, but I'm also thrilled." And a smile returned to her face, Susan seemed to be changing before my eyes.

"The key isn't in doing something. It's in being (or becoming) something. If you worked on doing, you are working at modifying your behavior. And eventually it becomes exhausting trying new behaviors all the time. Like starting an exercise program just because you feel like you should without an understanding of what you're trying to achieve. You tire and eventually conclude the behavior doesn't work.

"However, what you've just experienced is what we call a shift of your being," I said calmly. "You don't 'do' 'presence.' You just are present. It's a difference between you trying (and faking) being present and just seeing yourself as a 'present person.' Once you've experienced this internal shift of yourself, you see how protecting your emotional reserves is paramount to your thriving; you have shifted your being. And once that has happened, you won't consider your attitude a performance because it's part of who you are. Less doing, more being. Yeah, it's harder than it sounds. That's what I mean when I remind you that you're first a human BEING—not a human DOING."

"Do you ever reach a point where 'being' brings the same rush as 'doing'?" she asked.

I smiled, caught a little off guard by the straightforwardness of the question. She had brought the conversation to a philosophical place, and I loved it. So, encouraging her to go further, I asked, "What 'rush' are you speaking of?"

It was a familiar sentiment. Most reactive high achievers are driven by that same rush—the feeling of accomplishment, the recognition, the numbers going up. Susan's question was more insightful than she realized. But I didn't want to be presumptuous and wanted her to think through her own realization.

"You know, like having the inbox with NO emails in it, or finally crossing off the last item on my to-do list before going home for the night. That sort of rush. Like the Zen I've been chasing has finally arrived."

"It might be helpful to learn something about physiology for a minute, so indulge me as I finally get to put some of my master's degree to use," I said jovially.

"When we learn something new, the brain gives us a little reward to help us lock in what we learned. It's a chemical called dopamine. It's natural, and it's designed to help us continue to learn. It's the same molecule that helps a rat learn the maze to find the reward at the end. And each time we put the rat in the maze, they learn how to run just a little faster by avoiding a wrong turn so they can get to the reward faster. And ultimately, get to the dopamine hit faster. In the course of your leadership career and life experiences, you've learned a lot, for sure. And dopamine has been involved all along that journey. Yet when you drain your brain and deplete your reserves, it craves a hit. It is telling you to go learn something so you'll get your reward. Or it could be telling you that you need to run the rat race faster and faster to get to the reward before someone else takes it. And the more depleted your reserves are, the more your brain screams for the hit, craving that feeling of energy dopamine brings. Before you know it, you've literally rewired your brain and are in full-fledged dopamine addiction. Perhaps that's the 'rush' you're describing?"

Susan looked away, looking uncomfortable.

"But you also experience other chemicals, and you can use them to rewire your brain if you learn how to," I said.

"When we experience pleasurable moments—looking at the sunset, seeing a new puppy, appreciating fine art, or after a tense but meaningful conversation with a loved one, for example, the brain releases other chemicals known as endorphins and serotonin. These chemicals are responsible for a sensation of bliss or serenity. They can provide more than a "rush"; they can provide us with a feeling of lasting significance. And this sensation increases our resilience, even in the midst of the rat race, not in spite of it."

Susan smiled before interjecting. "It sounds like dopamine is a bit like fast food. Like going through the McDonald's drive-thru. It's quick, it's delicious, and it gives you an immediate reward. But the thing with fast food is that it leaves you hungry not long after. When I do that, my brain tells me to go back for more, so you keep going through the drive-thru. It sustains in the short term, but it doesn't help to thrive in the long term."

I chuckled, nodding in agreement. "I see where you're going with this.

"Yes, and on the other hand," I said, "reward chemicals like endorphins and serotonin come into play when you experience moments of purpose and peace. Think about the 'runner's high' that comes after miles of running. It's not instant gratification and requires a bit of effort to achieve this state, but it lasts. Rather than the drive-thru meal, it's more like nourishing, well-cooked food. It leaves you full, satisfied, and peaceful.

"Serotonin and endorphins take us to that place of 'flow,' a state of being where everything feels right, and our minds and bodies are in harmony. Where we find ourselves getting lost in time and truly enjoying the hard work that is happening to achieve this state. It's the difference between living for the next achievement and living in alignment with our deeper purpose. We don't get that quick rush, but the lasting peace. We breathe slower, feel grounded, and we don't need the next 'hit' to feel whole."

Susan was visibly intrigued. "So, that's what I'm missing," she said thoughtfully. "I get the dopamine from the quick wins, but the deeper, lasting peace—that's what I'm after."

I nodded.

Let's put it in real terms. "When you check something off the list, it feels rewarding. But when you're with your kids (or maybe even an employee) and you're helping them become better leaders in the world, you're achieving your more existential purpose," I expanded. "You will nearly always default to doing something by yourself that gives you a quick hit because you feel more in control of that, and you know what success looks like. But when you're mentoring your kids or your employees, it's more nebulous. It's undefined, and you may not have a concrete sense of accomplishment. But over time, when you see them being better citizens in the world and achieving their own unique purpose, you will have a lasting sense of satisfaction knowing you lived your calling for legacy and connection."

When we give in to temporary acts of heroism, we'll feel like we ran away and cheapened that sense of legacy.

"Which do you want more of? Which do you want less of?" I asked, not requiring a response.

We're all designed to be creative, to bring something meaningful into the world. When we feel stuck or unfulfilled, it's often because we're chasing the wrong rewards. I could see that this is exactly where Susan was. She might be making more money, growing her businesses, and adding more possessions, but she was really searching for something deeper. She was searching for the thing only she could create in this world and that she was uniquely best at.

She leaned back in her chair, her mind clearly working through the implications.

"Because at the end of the day, it's not the money, the cars, or the houses that will define your legacy. It's the moments when we are fully present, fully engaged in our purpose—whether that's with family, work, or within ourselves," I emphasized.

Susan looked at me in realization.

So, I continued. "If it strokes your ego, it gives you that quick dopamine hit. It's okay every now and then, but if that's all you're constantly chasing, you'll always be hungry for more. But if it feeds your soul, if it aligns with your deeper purpose, it brings you peace. That's what lasts."

She nodded, taking it in. "So, when I'm faced with a decision— whether it's a late-night meeting or a chance to close a deal—the real question is: does this stroke my ego or feed my soul?"

"That's it," I said, feeling the moment resonate between us.

Susan sat quietly for a few moments, reflecting. "It's different for everyone, isn't it? Some people chase productivity, others chase acceptance and affirmation, or being the smartest person in the room. But the ones who are truly happy, they're the ones who enjoy the simple things."

I nodded. "That's right. The happiest people aren't necessarily the ones with the most "stuff"—they're the ones who have found a way to live in alignment with their purpose. They've learned to be, rather than always needing to do."

As Susan put away her notes in preparation to log off, I could see the shift in her demeanor. She was leaving with a new perspective, one that would guide her choices in the days, weeks, and years to come. She smiled as she logged off the call, and I knew that today's conversation had left a lasting impact.

Another good session had come to a close. I reflected on our conversation knowing that she was on the path toward something greater—something far more fulfilling and lasting. And that was a victory in itself.

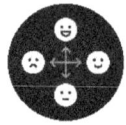

· CHAPTER SEVEN ·

EMOTIONS AS ADVENTURE GUIDES NOT DESTINATION DICTATORS

The sun filtered gently through the office windows, casting long, warm beams across the room. It was one of those crisp mornings that hinted at the start of a beautiful day. But we had barely settled in our seats when Susan asked, with an unusual urgency, "Is it this difficult for everyone?"

I smiled at her question, knowing she was wrestling with something familiar to so many people at a certain stage of life. "It's not just you, Susan," I began. "It's a philosophical tension, sure, but it's also tied to age, experience, and a shift in what we think success looks like. In our 20s, we're usually out to prove something—to show our strength, our capabilities. Whether it's how we handle relationships or how we treat others, we're trying to find out who we are in relation to the world."

She nodded, so I continued. "Then, by the time we hit our 30s, it's more about accumulation. The more we can gather—money, success, titles, relationships—the better we think we're doing. But then, as we get older, somewhere in our 40s, the game changes. The dopamine hits from those earlier pursuits stop having the same effect. The adrenaline rush fades. We start wondering, 'What now?' We've got the house, the car, the spouse, the accolades. We've ticked all the boxes. But the question becomes: What more is there? What do I really want now?"

Susan looked at me thoughtfully. "Peace," she said with a slightly sarcastic tone. "Although it sounds like I'm competing in a queen pageant, I want lasting peace. I truly do."

"Exactly. Somewhere around our 40s, something shifts, and most of us start wondering, 'Is there more?' Simultaneously, we are bombarded with increased responsibilities. We probably earned a promotion or two, the kids are getting older, our parents are aging, civic organizations beckon us to serve, etc.

"We crave a more efficient way to live and yet can feel trapped because the more we do what we've already done, the more we'll get from what we have. And most do not want more time debt, frustration, or confusion. At this point, we're really craving joy, peace, meaning, connection and bliss. But those are 'being' states, not 'doing' states. That's the difference. Not everyone gets to this stage, though. A lot of people keep living in that reactive state, navigating life by the rules they've created over time, repeating the same cycles. But there's a small percentage that make the leap—they fight the tension. They start authoring their own lives."

Susan rested her chin on her hand, her eyes distant. "So, you're saying most people don't even understand this tension? They just go through life reacting?"

"Well, I think most recognize something is different. Some call it a midlife crisis and try to wait it out. Others might realize that things are wrong and try to work harder, faster, longer, or cheaper, burying themselves in the grave of depleted energy. And there are a few who wake up and realize this is the chrysalis that will fundamentally change the way they go about leading the rest of their lives."

Susan was rapt and paying attention to every word I was saying.

"Chrysalis. Yes!" she repeated and then asked, "How do some make it through while others stall out?"

"The difference is in how well they are able to use their emotions as adventure guides versus letting them be the destination dictators.

"Many people don't even recognize their emotions, let alone understand them. Take men, for example—when I ask them what they are feeling, they'll usually respond with 'fine'—which isn't even an emotion. It's a combination of all the emotions averaged into one word. When pressed, they can usually say they feel anger, sadness, and maybe even happiness. But they don't often name more than 4-5 emotions. Emotions like grief, shame, fear, or even loneliness get buried. Why? Because too many boys have been told to 'rub some dirt on it' or called hurtful names when they expressed their pain. So, going into the future they've learned to distance themselves from those emotions because of not wanting to jeopardize the sense of belonging or community they desire most."

I thought quietly to myself about the many men I've worked with. I've seen how most men also recall how they made stupid decisions when feeling strong emotions—something they said or did in the spur of the moment so they bury their emotions under the single word 'fine'. On average, women may be slightly better at naming emotions, but it's a far cry from the full spectrum that is involved with the human experience. With that thought I brought myself back to Susan and her reflection.

"However, the depth of your emotions is what connects you to your soul," I said. "That's why humans can recall a blissful moment like the birth of a baby or the first time they hit a home run. Likewise, most can recall vivid details about a tragic moment like losing a loved one or being shamed when they were only a small child. The deep emotional experiences are what make life feel real and truly what connect us as humans.”

Susan looked out the window as if searching for something in the distance. "When I'm not being productive, I don't feel good. It's like my brain is wired to keep me busy. It's hard to sit still or even take a break. We are all wired to crave the dopamine hit, right?”

I smiled, sensing that we were about to dig into something even more interesting. "Not exactly," I said. "You are still in control of your brain. Our brain isn't naturally wired to equate being industrious with being productive. You've allowed your brain to crave those hits of dopamine. We have already talked about dopamine as the reward chemical.

“When you get your project done or complete the task, and you get praised, a little dopamine gets released. And you feel good. But you don't get praised for every task you do, so you've learned that the more tasks you complete, the more likely you are to get your reward. It's similar to why drug addicts keep going back for more—it's not that their brains were naturally addicted to the drug. They learned to crave it because it gave them that rush. A kind of feeling. And once they got hooked, their physiology changed, and their bodies kept demanding more.”

Susan shifted in her chair.

"When you're constantly productive, you feel valuable, and your brain learns to pattern itself around that feeling. And when you stop, you feel a kind of withdrawal. That's why you feel restless when you deliberately avoid being busy. Your brain is craving its next fix.”

Susan nodded thoughtfully. "Now it makes sense why you said earlier that I can rewire my brain," she said. "I guess I'm going to have to chase rewards from something deeper, something more sustainable, something closer aligned to my purpose."

"And that starts with recognizing your emotions and being in tune with why you feel the way you do."

"That's the harder bit, isn't it?" she muttered.

"It is," I agreed. "But the alternative is to keep chasing that quick fix. It's like the rat in the maze going faster and faster, chasing the same reward and getting bored in the process. Only as humans, my clients often come to me with a feeling of being 'stuck' or 'in a rut.' And all they know is they want to get out—and fast."

When this is happening, we need to recognize we're trading long-term peace for short-term satisfaction. Once we start recognizing these emotions, we can begin to make different choices. We can choose the harder but more fulfilling path. It might be uncomfortable at first, but in the long run, it brings lasting peace.

Susan was silent for a while. "So, how does one start? How do you learn to choose the healthy way?"

"You start by getting in touch with what truly makes you feel alive. Think about those moments when you've felt real joy—not just the satisfaction of ticking off a to-do list, but the kind of joy that fills your whole being. Maybe it's spending time with your husband, James, or having a heart-to-heart with your kids. Maybe it's being in nature or simply allowing yourself to rest. Or maybe it's when you tackled that hard conversation with an underperforming employee and came out with a stronger relationship and better performance. Whatever it is, those moments are the ones you need to prioritize, to chase more, and then eliminate the busyness that masks itself as productivity."

Susan exhaled deeply, a look of clarity crossing her face. "It goes deeper than me being present. It's about learning where my emotions have prevented me from being present," she said, almost to herself. "I want to be present. For James, for my kids, for the people I care about."

I nodded. "And being present is uncomfortable work. It requires you to be in tune with your emotional state. When something is arising that is taking you away from being present, you need to attend to the emotion and return to your intention of being present. If being 'unproductive' is hijacking your ability to be present, you'll likely feel agitation or regret. Noticing this emotion and naming it will help you return to a present state of being where you can remind yourself that investing into your relationships is another form of productivity for a much higher goal than you previously had for yourself. Learn to talk to your emotions as the little tyrants they can be and learn to boss them around, instead of them directing what you do and don't do."

I explained what one of my clients shared with me. She relayed a story where, at 5:00, she was headed out to catch her daughter's softball game. She remembered she needed to send a message to her boss about the upcoming board meeting with an attachment she could only get from her computer. She started to feel agitated and then anxious. Realizing her emotions were taking over, she spoke to them, "I feel you, agitation. I hear you, anxiety. I know you want me to focus on getting that dopamine hit to make me feel better, but sending this email is only going to make me feel more regret from being late to the game. So, I'm choosing joy. I'm choosing to send this message in the morning."

Susan chuckled softly. "I like how you've explained emotions with science. Up till now I thought all the emotions stuff was just ... you know... too 'squishy.'"

I smiled. "It really is science—physical and emotional science! Our brain budgets our energy for our survival, not our thriving."

When tigers and lions are hunting you, it's helpful to have your brain shunt energy away from some areas toward others so you have the energy to escape and survive. But rarely are we being chased by lions and tigers. Our brain perceives threats of any sort nearly the same. Our emotional system sends the signal to the nervous system and triggers it for survival. When we feel negative emotions like fear or shame, the brain reads that as a threat— to our self-image, and the brain pulls resources away from some of our "executive functioning," like decision-making and rational thought, and helps us get to safety in the fastest way possible. If this happens on the rare occasion, it is manageable, but if someone is constantly in threat-detection mode, the nervous system wears out. Humans languish when all we do is survive.

Survival forces us to safety. But to truly feel alive we must do more than survive. We must thrive. And thriving demands that we live out our purpose. Safety and purpose are always in tension with one

> **Humans languish when all we do is survive.**

another. If you don't learn how to control it, your brain will always pull you into safety. So, you have to train it to be pulled towards purpose. When you let your emotions hijack your decisions and pull you toward safety, you are giving them complete control over your future. Yet, as you learn to speak into your emotions and start bossing them around, you regain your power to author the future you desire regardless of how you feel. And behind your emotions are all of the brain chemicals we've talked about. Playing it safe sometimes gives you the dopamine hit. But stepping into purpose— that gives you all the hits—dopamine, serotonin, and endorphins! What a rush!

You'll feel uncomfortable at first, maybe even restless, as your emotions start screaming. They start recruiting their friends, the Belief Bullies and the Dream Demons. These voices in your head and the negative feelings all over your body are there trying to convince you to go back to safety. But over time, as you prove to yourself you can do hard things, your brain adjusts. It starts learning what real threats to your survival look like. You wean off of the dopamine addiction, which helps your emotions, and your actions start proving to those belief bullies that they can rest and are safe, so they quiet down. Soon one hard thing becomes two, and then three, and now you've strung together a habit of facing the hard things and accomplishing meaningful stuff. Then you'll find more peace and joy in whatever threat you're facing. You don't have to give up the success you've enjoyed now just to get the peace you desire. It's not an either/or. It can be an and/both.

"Now you're really messing with me," said Susan. "I've always thought that I'll work hard now and enjoy peace later on vacation or in retirement. But now I see that that's just not true. If I still have my health in retirement—which, after all this stress, is very questionable—I may still not be weaned off my dopamine addiction. This explains why even on vacation I feel like I must keep up with the office, and when that doesn't work, I try to purposely leave my phone at home, but then I'm so irritable I feel like I ruin whatever we are doing."

"Yes, Susan," I affirmed.

In my life I've certainly seen a lot of retirees who expected to find peace in their golden years, but instead they found melancholy and boredom because their brain hadn't reoriented around what true success means. Even in retirement they are still in threat detection and dopamine addiction mode. Instead of missing out on the big meeting or the threat of missing out on the promotion, they are now fearful of running out of money, poor health, government instability, you name it—the threats are still there. Only now are they struggling with what to do to get their next dopamine hit with the pressures of the office or career removed. I was determined to help Susan avoid this situation in her own life.

Susan's face was reflecting a mix of hope and hesitation. "I think I get it. But how do I stop myself from falling back into old patterns? Like, if I need to have a hard conversation with James about something personal, but which could lead to more endorphins. Or if I have a business meeting, that feels easier; that would give me the quick hit. It's like I'm wired to choose the easier option."

"That's a common dilemma," I said. "When faced with two options—one that feels hard and one that feels easy—we usually choose the easier path. But here's the key: when you choose the harder path, you fall in the right direction. When you have that tough conversation with James, it might be uncomfortable at first. But in the long run, it will bring you closer to him and allow your relationship to blossom. It will bring you peace. On the other hand, choosing the easier option—the business meeting—might give you a quick hit of dopamine, but it is likely a distraction to your lasting fulfillment."

"Falling in the right direction," Susan repeated thoughtfully. "That's a good way to put it."

> **When you choose the harder path, you fall in the right direction.**

"Exactly. And the more you practice choosing the hard path—the path that brings you closer to your purpose—the easier it becomes. You start to rewire your brain to crave those deeper, more fulfilling experiences. And before you know it, those moments of joy, peace, and bliss start to outweigh the fleeting satisfaction of a job well done, for example."

Susan smiled, her face softening. "You break it down so simply."

"It's rewarding," I said, "but not easy. But you've already taken the first step, Susan. You're recognizing the tension. You're starting to question what really matters to you. And that's the beginning of change."

After summarizing what insights she gained on the call, she took a deep breath. "Thank you, Jim," she said. "I think I've got some real work to do. Not the kind that gets me accolades, but the kind that brings me peace."

"The pursuit of purpose and legacy is when we create and live inside our values. That's how you find peace," I concluded.

· CHAPTER EIGHT ·

CHOOSING YOUR "HARD"

The clock struck 8:00 a.m. on a cold Wednesday morning. The frost clung to the windows, and the early rays of sunlight were weak, struggling to break through the mist.

I sat at my desk and reviewed the notes from our previous conversation. I saw the notification that Scott had just joined our session, so I admitted him to the call. He was bundled up in a gray sweater, his face carrying the unmistakable weight of fatigue. It had been a few weeks since we last spoke, and from the looks of it, he had been reflecting on our previous conversations. As we settled into the conversation, it became clear what had been occupying his mind.

He sighed heavily. "Jim, I've been thinking a lot about my life—what retirement would look like, what the future holds once I no longer have to rush out the door for work every morning. What will be left when all is said and done?"

It was a poignant question, one that many successful professionals grapple with as they approach a different season of life. Scott was an accomplished accountant, liked by his peers and colleagues, yet there was a deeper question gnawing at him. What would he be remembered for, especially by the people who should matter most—his wife, Jessica, and their children?

That opening statement encapsulated the crux of his dilemma. Scott had a clear and meticulous work routine, one that his wife was fully aware of. His day began early and ended late, and as the years passed, those late nights became more frequent. He had become a fixture in the office but a ghost in his own home. Jessica had voiced her displeasure many times, yet Scott seemed trapped in the very ambition that had once driven him.

"Jessica isn't pleased with my late nights, Jim," Scott continued, his tone almost pleading for understanding. "But what am I supposed to do? Society expects a man to provide for his family. That's how we're measured—how we're valued. How else can I live up to that?"

The tension in his voice was palpable. This was a man at war with himself, torn between societal expectations and the growing unrest in his home. Scott was seeking guidance, but more importantly, he was seeking clarity.

"The challenge you're facing is about how to prioritize what is important versus what feels urgent?" I asked.

He nodded in agreement. "Exactly. The urgent things keep piling up. At work, we've just been introduced to a new advanced accounting software solution. My job is to make sure the senior and junior accountants know how to use it, and it's taking up a lot of my time."

Scott launched into a lengthy explanation about how the new software was crucial for their accounting firm, Zine Group, a huge conglomerate with more than 20 accountants at its headquarters alone. He had been tasked with overseeing the training sessions and ensuring a smooth transition to the new system. On top of that, Scott had been attending high-level strategy meetings with other CFOs, discussing how the software would be rolled out across all branches. There was a hard deadline for full integration, which only added to the pressure.

"I had to give up weekends to get everyone up to speed," Scott admitted. "It's eating into my personal time, but there's no other way."

"Had to?" I asked, as I let the impact of noticing his word choice hang in the air.

He shook his head. "You caught me again. I mean, I *chose* to give up my weekends to get everyone up to speed. I know essentially, I need to keep myself in the center of my decisions, but it didn't really feel like a choice. Who else was going to do it? And everyone around me is expecting me to get the implementation correct."

"And if this software project didn't exist, would you still find something to keep you at work late into the night?" I inquired.

Scott hesitated before responding, as if the answer had never occurred to him. "I keep thinking—hoping—that when I get whatever project or task I'm working on done, I'll have more time to dedicate to Jessica and the family," he said, though his tone lacked conviction. "My wife would say I'm always busy, no matter what. If it's not work, it's family or friends needing help with something, but I really don't see another way."

As Scott spoke, it became clear that his over-commitment to work and others wasn't just about this software project. It was a pattern— one that had served him well in climbing the corporate ladder but was now creating cracks in his personal life.

"So, what's the core issue here?" I asked.

"The time I'm losing with my family," Scott answered, the realization settling deeper into his mind. "And the fact that they aren't getting younger, and quite frankly neither am I."

I got the impression that Scott hadn't yet come to see that his methods weren't working for him. He wasn't quite ready to change. I earnestly wanted to help Scott see the distinction between needs and values, seeing how much that distinction had helped Susan. I wanted him to see how living out of alignment was constantly draining his reserves. Yet I could tell that he was not ready for more models, frameworks, or teaching. He needed to come to his own decisions about where to go. He had relied on others' opinions way too much, and one more suggestion from me might just give him another reason to comply while still lacking personal commitment to his growth journey.

"Jessica's been frustrated," Scott continued. "She's always telling me that we don't spend enough time together. She wants us to go on dates again and take family vacations. I want that too, but it feels like there's never enough time. Now that the kids are older, she wants to travel more. To see the world. She is no longer content with how things are."

I leaned in and asked the question that had been on my mind since we began. "Scott, if Jessica weren't upset about your late nights, would this be an issue for you?"

His face dropped slightly, and the answer came slower this time. "I think it would be," he admitted. "I guess I just haven't realized how big of a problem it is until now."

Scott was beginning to see what Jessica had been pointing out all along. The implications of the traits that had propelled him up the corporate ladder—his willingness to always say yes, his desire to be seen as competent and reliable—were now becoming a barrier to the life he said he wanted. Though on a deeper level, it seemed he wanted the life everyone else wanted him to have, and it was becoming increasingly obvious he couldn't please everyone.

I could tell this was uncomfortable for him, but it was important that he grapple with it.

"It seems to me that you've taken on the responsibility of overseeing this project, even though you're not directly involved in the training sessions," I said. "Is there a way to get this project done without you being on hand all the time?"

Scott thought for a moment. "I could step back from some of the sessions, sure. But I don't know how the CEO would feel about that. She's counting on me to make sure this transition goes smoothly."

"If you did that, it might ease your workload," I pointed out, "but it might not change the mindset that's driving you to overextend yourself. You seem to attach your value and worth to how much you can accomplish for others, how many 'thumbs up' you get—whether from your boss or your colleagues."

Scott shifted in his chair, running a hand through his hair. Defensively he spoke up, "I don't think that's fair. I am my own person. I decide what I want to do and when. Yet, I have a big job. And I need to do it well. And my boss is the one who determines if I do it well. But isn't that what we're all supposed to do? In Corporate America, the more you do and the more you can support teams, the more valuable you are. That's how you climb to the top."

"I don't know, Scott. That sounds like the way you've chosen to define success in Corporate America. There could be many other ways to define success as well. I do know that executive leadership requires many different skills than what got you to the C-suite in the first place. Are you willing to shift?"

As the conversation unfolded, it became clear that Scott's malaise wasn't just a side effect of his job and working too much; it was the result of a deeper issue. His sense of self-worth was tied to his ability to be "the man who always delivered." From childhood, Scott had been rewarded for being likable, agreeable, and dependable. Over the years, he had built his identity around that image, continuously striving to meet the expectations of others.

Without a shift in his identity, any behavior or skill he tried to develop would only be adding to his frustration. He fundamentally needed to see himself differently and grow toward that identity.

"If you want to shift this dynamic, Scott, you're going to have to change how you see yourself," I explained. "You need to start finding value in areas that go beyond your own individual accomplishments. You got here because you can get a lot done, and you're still relying on that set of skills to keep you here. But now it's about systems, cultures, building leadership, and strategy—all things that transcend the self and impact the bigger picture. If you continue to base your worth on whether or not you're in your boss's good graces, you'll always feel pressured to prioritize pleasing others—especially others with power of evaluation over you—over the things that you want to achieve in life or become. You need to be ready to disrupt your old sense of identity."

"I know you're right," Scott said, sighing heavily. "But it's hard."

"It is hard to shift, yes," I said. "But to be candid, it also seems hard to stay where you are at. Each session you come in more dejected, looking for answers from me."

I disclosed to Scott that I noticed a pattern that I'd hoped would change over time, but still had not after months of working together. I always started our sessions with, "What do you want to accomplish today?" And most times he didn't have a clear answer or a firm direction on what he was choosing to do to move toward his goals and what was holding him back. He would launch into a long conversation with a status update on a project or a review he had just conducted, and seemed to hope that I would have some words of wisdom or insights that would help him feel better.

Growing into the leader you were meant to be is a lifetime journey, but it is an adventure. The adventure toward the growth you're looking for is the adventure within. One where you must do lots of soul searching, evaluation, reprioritization, and ultimately standing in your own unique power—not looking to your right or your left for validation. And feeling the belonging you desire not because others have affirmed you, but because you know that what you bring to the world is a gift that is absolutely needed and others want. Then you authentically belong and find the community you are so desperately trying to be a part of.

"Growing is hard. But staying the same is hard too. Which 'hard' do you choose?" I asked.

Scott was quiet for a moment, his expression introspective. I could see him wrestling with the conflict—taking full responsibility for his life, including his professional accomplishments and his personal life, versus his need for external validation. The realization was beginning to dawn on him, and he was becoming aware of the long road ahead.

> **Growing is hard. But staying the same is hard too.**

"What do you think the difference is between things that are urgent and things that are important?" I asked, wanting him to dig deeper into this realization.

Scott rested his elbows on his knees as he considered the question. "To me, urgent things feel like they have a deadline," he said.

"They're pressing, immediate. But important things... Those are lasting. They don't have a deadline, but they're the things that matter most to us in the long run. My family, for instance. They're important. But I keep pushing them aside because work always feels more urgent."

I nodded. "In the truest definition, the distinguishing factor between what is urgent and what is important is our perception of time."

I explained further that urgent things often feel like they have a fixed timeframe, like a software launch or a project deadline. They create a sense of immediate pressure. But the important things—the eternal ones, like Scott's relationships with Jessica and his kids—don't have the same sense of urgency until something drastic happens; a crisis or a loss.

It is these moments that snap us out of our perception and readjust the definition of time. They remind us that time is fleeting, that we are only ephemeral. That we can move something that is eternal forward to be dealt with immediately. These moments can't be gotten back. It could be the kid's graduation, the death of a loved one, or a battle with a disease or diagnosis. Those kinds of moments make us realize, "Gosh, where have I been?" Our challenge is to alter our perception of time into that moment where we realize we're investing now because we don't know if tomorrow will come.

"I know Jessica sees it that way," Scott said. "She's always saying that we can't get these moments back. But I haven't been able to... I don't know... internalize that in the same way. I feel like I'll always have time to make up for the lost moments later. Isn't that what retirement is supposed to be for?"

"That's not for me to decide," I said. "What do you want your retirement to be about, Scott?" I allowed him a moment for reflection.

That's the trap many reactive leaders default to when they aren't in control. They think there's always time to make it right, but the truth is, time is fleeting. And when we finally wake up to that reality, sometimes it's too late to fix what's been broken. The key is to make the important things urgent now—before a crisis forces us to see it. But again, it's truly about you choosing. Choosing YOUR "hard."

I could observe that at this point, Scott was not ready to disrupt his old patterns of over-compliance. He hadn't decided to face the tension between finding his meaning and safety in structure and boundaries, and standing out in his own power, and finding the authentic belonging he so desperately desired. He remained caught in the cycle of continuing to look for external validation of his success instead of defining what success truly meant to him, and having the ability to actualize that success in the world.

As the session drew to a close, a heavy silence settled between us. Scott made it clear he had decided not to continue with leadership coaching.

"I think it's time for me to go," he said heavily. I knew that would be our last session.

The months of coaching thus far provided Scott with the awareness of how to get what he wanted out of life. It defined the bridge he would need to cross. Yet ultimately, he became fearful of exhibiting his own power. The future he wanted was just around the corner on Scott's "Adventure Within," but his fear of stepping into this adventure would put that future on hold—for now.

· CHAPTER NINE ·

TO BUILD BETTER HUMANS, YOU MUST GO FIRST

Mike

Noah, Mike's son, was in his final year at university. As usual, when Mike and I would begin a session, we started by catching up on family. Mike was excited because Noah was coming home for the holidays. But the more immediate event on Mike's mind was his upcoming visit to Noah's college the following week, where his son would be participating in the 400m hurdles during the college trials. Mike's voice lit up as he spoke about Noah.

Although our sessions usually revolved around leadership and personal growth, moments like these—when Mike opened up about his family—always felt like a breakthrough. His relationships with his children, particularly Noah, had been a sticking point for a long time. But over the course of our coaching relationship, Mike had made tremendous strides in rebuilding those bonds.

When he and I first began working together, Mike had admitted that his children often felt that he was more like a boss than a father. He regretted the disconnect he felt with them emotionally and was often agitated by what he considered "poor choices" they were making. But now, he was starting to see his role as more of a guide— someone who could help his children navigate their own paths without controlling or dictating to them what he wanted them to do.

Coaching had provided Mike with the awareness that his reliance on his intellect allowed him to live in judgement of others' actions and choices. With that awareness, he decided to practice curiosity, realizing that even if he would have made a different decision, his children were learning to live their own lives with their choices, bringing rewards or consequences to themselves. He no longer felt that he needed to come up with the answers and tell them what to do. This shift in perspective had led to real improvements, and Mike was feeling more connected to his family than ever before.

Once we had caught up on his family, we moved on to the topic of the day—Mike's reflections on who he wanted to be, not just to his family but to his friends and the people in his life. He revealed that while his relationships with his children were improving, he felt a deep dissatisfaction with his friendships.

"As I get further into this adventure, I realize I need deeper relationships with people inside and outside of work to help sustain me. Right now, I'm struggling with my relationships with my friends, Jim," Mike admitted, his demeanor changing. "I've invested so much of my time into work, building my career, and recently into my family. But it feels like my friendships have become surface-level, you know? Not deep, not meaningful."

This wasn't the first time Mike had mentioned feeling disconnected from his social circle, but today he seemed more reflective about it. Mike believed that relationships should play a central role in his purpose, yet he was frustrated because he didn't feel drawn to deepening the friendships he currently had.

He paused, as if trying to find the right words. "It's like... I know relationships will play a prominent role in helping me live my purpose continually, but I don't know if the ones I have are worth pursuing anymore. It feels like there's no depth to them. And the truth is, I don't know if I even have the time or energy to fix that.

"Do I try to grow them, or do I let them go?" he asked.

Mike's sense of purpose, in the last few months since we began this coaching relationship, had shifted from being successful and efficient in business, to helping others be more successful in business and life. He had recognized that his journey to a more joyful position of leadership was to first become a better human himself—to be more content with himself and his gifts. He wanted others to experience the joy and freedom he had found, which he believed would help them become better humans themselves.

And so, he wanted deeper and more meaningful friendships which would support him on this continued adventure within.

Mike's face revealed the conflict within him. As CEO of First Lead Technology Ltd., his work consumed most of his time. In recent months, he had made a conscious effort to carve out more time

> **To build better humans, you must go first.**

for his immediate family. Yet, the pressure of maintaining relationships beyond that often left him feeling drained. He found himself responding to friends' invitations with hesitation, unsure if they had the emotional bandwidth to engage in the deep conversations he now desired.

"How can relationships be part of my purpose if I'm not excited about them anymore?" Mike asked, a note of frustration in his voice.

I leaned back, considering his words. "If I understand correctly, you believe that your relationships are a key factor in you living for more significance and closer to your purpose, but now that you've grown closer to your family, you're questioning if investing in your existing friendships will bring you closer to or further from fulfilling that purpose. Is that right?"

Mike nodded. "Exactly. But more than that, I feel like I'm a different person. A person on a great adventure toward something really great but often, the travelers around me are more wandering, content to stay the same and often grumbling because they don't see anything better than it is today. I guess I just don't want to deal with any more shallow connections. I want some adventure partners."

This was where the tension lay. Mike craved deeper, more meaningful relationships but wasn't sure if his current friends were the ones that could give him that. He was visibly torn between maintaining these relationships and his growing need for personal alignment with his values.

"A group of friends I've known for years reached out recently," Mike said. "They want to meet up in Dallas for a hangout, but my immediate reaction wasn't excitement. It was more like, 'How am I going to deal with this?'"

I could see the weariness in his eyes. As someone who had now begun to value his personal time, Mike had become more protective of it now than before. The idea of spending it in social settings, splashed with alcohol and loud conversations, no longer brought the joy it once had.

"What is it that you desire out of these friendships that would make them feel like part of your purpose?" I asked.

"I want people to notice the changes I'm making and be curious about them," he replied. "I want to share my story and impact them in some way. I want them to see who I've become and more broadly, I want them to find what I found—purpose beyond providing, like my life is actually creating something that was always meant to be. I'm just not sure that's possible with my old friends."

There was a moment of silence during which Mike reflected.

"How can I be drawn to something and feel disinterested by it at the same time?" Mike asked, frustrated.

"That's the tension you're grappling with," I responded. "What is it about these friendships that drains your energy?"

"I think it's the superficiality of it all," Mike admitted. "When we meet up, it's always the same—talking about work, gossiping about old acquaintances, nothing really meaningful. It just feels like a drain on my battery."

"And what relationships replenish your battery?" I asked.

"My family," Mike said without hesitation. "Spending time with them is never a waste. Whether it's having dinner, watching a movie, playing a game, or going on vacation, I always feel recharged. I don't regret a single second with them."

"Are there others that bring you energy?" I asked.

Mike drifted away in thought for a bit before sharing a story about an up-and-coming engineer, Lindsay, he had met in one of the employee town halls. In this young talent, Mike saw himself. Bright, intelligent and sometimes over-reliant on her own smarts. She was getting results but in her quest to be right, was also adding a lot of friction to her relationships.

For the last five weeks, Mike had been intentional to have lunch with this potential star for the business. "After our meetings, I feel like I could walk on the moon!" exclaimed Mike. "The conversations are sometimes unnerving because she's asking me about how I learned to grow to the leader I am, and I have to answer authentically, by sharing with her my story about how I had to DISRUPT, BRIDGE and GROW continuously. This involves sharing some of my 'not so famous' moments too, if you know what I mean."

It was becoming clear to both of us that Mike was in a different phase of life now. He had come a long way, and his perspective on relationships had shifted. Where once he might have valued the camaraderie of his friends, now he was more selective about where he spent his energy.

"Mike, I think you're in a different place now," I said. "You've grown, and you're more intentional about where you invest your time and energy. Here's how I explain it. You've taken on your own adventure within. And as a result, you're becoming a better human. You see the freedom and joy this journey has afforded you. Now, because you went first, you want others to find what you've found. You're able to help others embark on their own journey."

Mike nodded thoughtfully.

I continued. "When we reach this phase in life, we start auditing our time. We measure the impact that certain activities will have on us. Sometimes, we crave connection, but not necessarily the investment of time it requires. In those cases, maybe it's not about hanging out physically but about finding ways to connect that align with who you are now. A phone call or virtual meeting could be enough to maintain relationships and to love people where they are at. You don't need to let the relationship go, but you do need to allow it space to grow. And growth will not happen—no matter how much you want it to—until that person decides they must take their own steps toward growth."

I sat with that statement for a few seconds in silence, reflecting on Scott and hoping that even though he concluded his coaching, he was still continuing his own adventure within.

I collected my thoughts and returned to the conversation, "There are other relationships, as you've illustrated in the story of Lindsay, you're willing to give up some of your precious time to see a longer-term impact to what you're doing. Maybe even more existential in nature. These relationships must be invested into.

"The person is receptive and your wisdom is too rich not to share. A casual phone call may not be sufficient with these relationships. And candidly, the wisdom you gained through this adventure came with some significant costs—an expensive tuition bill. Don't you agree?"

Mike chuckled.

"So, you want to return the favor but only to those that are willing to receive that value and do something with it."

Mike sighed, as if a weight had been lifted. "I think you're right. I'm just not the same person I used to be. I've changed, and I'm not interested in the same things anymore. And I have a greater desire to help others with what I've learned."

"Some of your friends might be in a different place in life," I suggested. "But that doesn't mean the relationship has to end. Maybe you can connect with them in a way that aligns with your new values. If you approach them from where you are now, they might respond in a way that surprises you. Your friends may be looking for the same things as you, but they just don't know how to express it. Maybe they're engaging in those old lifestyles because it's what they know, but deep down, they're searching for more meaningful connections with the thought that those activities make them vulnerable enough."

Mike was quiet for a moment. "I guess I've been afraid of that—afraid that if I go back to those friendships, I'll slip into my old patterns. I don't want that."

"I doubt that is going to happen," I shared. "I've noticed a fundamental shift in the way you see yourself—a shift in your being. It's like you've crossed a threshold and the door to the "old Mike" closed behind you forever. You can't go back. Not with the way you see the world and your place in it today."

"You've grown, and your friendships can grow with you. At the same time, you also have the right—really the obligation—to set boundaries. You can say yes to the things that align with your values and no to the things that don't. That's how you avoid feeling drained and move closer and closer to living into your purpose. The adventure never stops as long as you're alive. If you're not dead, you're not done," I quipped, remembering my conversation with Susan.

Mike smiled. "I think that's it, Jim. I think I just didn't have the confidence in my new self yet and I was afraid I would regress if I continued my old friendships. But maybe I just need to give myself permission to be who I am now and let the chips fall where they may."

I smiled back. "Exactly. Your purpose is tied to who you are now, not who you used to be. And if those friendships no longer serve you, it's okay to let them go. But how can you keep these friendships and let them grow with you as you grow?"

Mike nodded, deep in thoughts, as he pondered the answer. "This has been really helpful. I think I know what I need to do now. It's up to them to accept the new me, and if they can't, then I'll find people who can."

"And that's okay," I said. "Just remember, when you say yes to the things that align with who you are now, you're living creatively toward a more purposeful existence, not reactively toward the same stuck feeling you had when we started this adventure together."

In my own journey I've had to learn to protect my purpose, and I've realized, if my decision is not a "hell yes" then it has to be a "hell no." This simple distinction has helped me stay grounded and present in ambiguity or competing priorities. It certainly has helped me see forward progress in my life and freedom to pursue my purpose. Candidly, it was a defining phrase I reflected on when leaving my corporate job. I wasn't sure what my future was, but I knew in my soul that saying "yes" to a mediocre job was going to keep me further away from finding my own "hell yes!" As we sat in silence, I could see Mike formulating his own boundary narrative.

> **If my decision is not a "hell yes" then it has to be a "hell no."**

We let that thought linger while our time together drew to a close. Neither wanted to say goodbye to the other; our coaching relationship was coming to an end.

Mike's journey was far from over, but I could see that a new chapter had begun. He was learning to let go of the old patterns that no longer served him, and to embrace the person he was becoming.

Over the next few years, I quietly observed First Lead Technology, Ltd. Their results were impressive. The company had completed multiple acquisitions and had out-performed investor expectations. I was very impressed. I would get an occasional phone call or email from Mike relaying his latest accomplishment. And when he reported success, rarely did he tell me about the financial performance of the company or the earnings per share his investors received. He almost always shared about an insight he had gained, a relationship he developed, or a new idea for the next non-profit he wanted to start.

I knew Mike was definitely on the highway in his own *Adventure Within*.

Susan

As I logged in for Susan's session that Tuesday morning, the change in her was immediately obvious. The joy she radiated was palpable, almost contagious. Her wide smile brightened her face, and there was an undeniable lightness to her demeanor that hadn't been there before.

"Where are we headed today?" Susan teased, echoing the way I typically began our conversations.

I smiled back. "You tell me," I said.

She paused for a moment, then replied, "Nothing much. I just think I understand now—more than I ever have—the importance of living within our values."

Susan had come to a powerful realization: she didn't have to cheapen or compromise her needs in order to get them met. Through our work together, particularly with the needs and values exercises, she had learned to prioritize what was truly important over what felt urgent. She was making conscious efforts to meet her needs in a way that aligned with her core values, rather than sacrificing her well-being just to meet the demands of others.

Before, Susan had been constantly trying to balance the conflicting pressures of work and family, juggling responsibilities and trying to keep everyone happy. But now something had shifted. She wasn't just seeking balance anymore; she was actively realigning her life to live in congruence with her values. She was striving to be the person she wanted to be, rather than the person she felt she had to be.

Over the months leading up to this session, Susan would regularly send me updates, sharing the progress she was making in becoming an empowered leader. It was incredible to witness. She had started setting firm boundaries with clients and colleagues, something she had struggled with before. Susan upheld new standards, and she delegated more responsibilities to her team, especially to the presidents of the ever-expanding companies in her empire, giving them the opportunity to take ownership of their roles and allowing her to step into leading this exploding enterprise.

By letting go of the need to micromanage every aspect of her business, Susan was transforming into a visionary leader. She no longer felt the need to control everything directly; instead, she empowered others to take on leadership roles, trusting them to make decisions without her constant oversight.

As she empowered these leaders with the responsibilities of running their businesses and learned how to appropriately hold them accountable, she was also subliminally guiding them in their own *Adventure Within*. Susan's leaders were now building teams and cultures based on the wisdom she'd gained by taking her own adventure toward becoming a better human. No longer did her leaders report problems with recruitment as people were flooding their inbox with resumes hoping to land a job at one of the companies she owned. No longer did she fret about cashflow—the results were better than she could have ever expected!

But it wasn't just her professional life that had improved. Susan made intentional time for her family and friends, carving out space in her life for the people who mattered most. She began to author this new version of herself, shaping her relationships and interactions around the person she wanted to be—someone who was present, purposeful, and grounded in her values.

She craved this sort of connection—true belonging– more than anything. She realized that for a long time, her desire for belonging was based on trying to earn it. But now it was about adding authentic value to people by helping them become a better human too. Of course, not everyone she knew was ready for this journey, but even in that she found growth. She had more patience and grace for people knowing that at some point, life would present enough challenges for them, that they would start asking the question, "Is this all?" and when they did, she was ready to assist them in their journey.

Of course, it wasn't always linear– up and to the right like the growth graphs of her companies. She wasn't perfect. There were moments, as she candidly admitted, when old patterns crept back in. She sometimes fell into the trap of overworking or feeling the need to manage every detail herself. But each time this happened, Susan would perform what she called a "self-audit." She would reflect on the situation, identify where her emotions had hijacked her adventure, where she had acted out of alignment with her values, and take intentional steps to correct it.

It was usually then that she'd drop me a text message and share with me, "growth is a journey, not a destination. I'm still on my adventure."

In one message, she relayed how this practice of self-awareness remained foundational in helping her optimize her life. She'd learned to embrace that phrase, forgoing the old "work/life balance" equation she'd held for so long. Balance implies things are just one decision away from falling apart. Optimization helped her have freedom to realize that it didn't all have to be equal and there were more than two things in conflict at any given time. She had to optimize her life to keep on this adventure.

Rather than beating herself up for falling back into old patterns, she learned to be compassionate with herself and view each moment as an opportunity for growth. Whenever she recognized a misstep and her resilience would start to wane, she realigned her actions with her values and moved forward with greater clarity and resolve.

Susan was honored for being the "entrepreneur of the year" by her state department of commerce. The growth of her businesses was helping the communities where they were founded revitalize— providing not only revenue and jobs for the local economies, but they were becoming a natural source of volunteer leaders who were engaging with local PTO clubs, Rotary clubs, civic and religious institutions. In her acceptance speech Susan recounted her *Adventure Within*. She recalled how she found the peace she had been seeking for so long. She no longer felt the constant pressure to control everything or the guilt for not being "perfect" or even the drain of constantly trying to earn her belonging. Instead, she had embraced a leadership style that allowed her to be both successful and true to herself. And she was amazed that she didn't have to give up growing her businesses to find what she most wanted.

She shared her wisdom with the audience, "I've realized that true leadership isn't about controlling others and amassing things based on a need for safety," she said, thoughtfully, "It's about living out your purpose and impacting your relationships in meaningful ways. It's about leading with integrity, staying true to your values, and being fully present in the moments that matter most."

She paused, as if letting the weight of her own words settle in. "I like who I'm becoming," she added, her voice filled with gratitude. "Thank you for this honor."

Susan had invited me to attend the dinner and ceremony, and I gladly accepted. Hearing those words was deeply rewarding. Susan's journey had been one of transformation, but it wasn't just about achieving professional success. It was much bigger than that. She was now having generational success multiplied through everyone who was blessed to meet her.

As I was flying home from that event, I couldn't help but feel proud of Susan's journey. She had discovered the power of true leadership —creative transformative leadership. She was more joyful, the world was becoming better, other humans were on their own *Adventure Within*, and I had never felt more in the center of my purpose, continuing my own Adventure!

· CHAPTER TEN ·

THE ADVENTURE WITHIN

I n the quieter moments of life, you can likely admit to hearing that little voice somewhere inside that beckons you to become more— to live a life of significance, not just pursue success. To move beyond providing a life for others, to living a life that matters. Your very being knows you were meant to create, not just consume. As a child you responded to this voice by trying to become "more" of whatever earned you affection. You might have become more likable, or more intellectual, or more productive. You did this, unknowingly, in an effort to feel more successful and therefore valued by the cruel world you didn't choose to belong to, but have chosen to respond to. Feeling successful and valued helped you discover your place in this world. This place in the world created a cheapened sense of belonging, and because it worked for you, you developed your identity around it. You learned to take pride in it and find safety.

Perhaps one day in this pursuit of safety and your childlike attempt to hold on to your place in the world, something went wrong or didn't result in what you intended. Maybe pain, disease or loss entered your world and you started wondering "is this all there is?" Maybe you found yourself realizing the way you are working is no longer working for you. And fear set in. Fear of what you're about to lose. And maybe fear of how far you have to go.

Here you are. Feeling loss, and feeling lost. Your uniqueness— and likely your gifts in this world— makes you feel isolated. For fear of being rejected from the "in crowd," you choose to hide your uniqueness. You become more of what you think allows you to fit in. You give others what you think they want from you. You grow in skills but not in wisdom. You continue to curate an environment that you perceive as safe because of what you do to earn your place. You build superficial relationships, your elite game of "hide and protect" garners. You realize— maybe after a downsizing, a death, or a divorce, that most of your relationships are built on a quid-pro-quo status— the more you do for them, the more they do for you. But now you're realizing you played the game, but your partner, employer or friend didn't have the same rules. Over time, as your responsibilities increase (family expands, career grows, society gets more complex), your mental health deteriorates as you're convinced you can't possibly do more to earn more. And now you're at a crossroads. *"How do I get more, without doing more?"* asks the weary leader in desperation.

The answer lies within your being. First and foremost, **you are a human being**. Not a human doing. You can't "do" your way into love or belonging. You were already created to belong. So, you have to realize how to be. You have to be loving. But you can't "be" loving when you're trying to earn love. You can't be present when you're trying to earn presence. You can't be valued when you're trying to earn your value. Said more simply, you can't keep reacting to life around you. You have to start creating the life you want to have by being the person you were designed to be.

Most of the clients I work with will wrestle with a nagging sense that they are missing the hallmark of their lives. At one point or another, they start to realize they've been pursuing success at the expense of significance. Most will admit they have achieved success by learning the rules around them and playing the game better than most. Essentially, they've mastered the game played out on the reality TV show "Survivor" by outwitting, outlasting and outplaying while creating superficial alliances that should protect them from the inevitable 'Tribal Council' vote where they might realize their mortal fear – being voted off the island (or out of a job!). In this pursuit they've realized the "significant" things of life have become threadbare. When pressed, most will define significance by using words like "meaning," "purpose," "connection" or "legacy." These are the things most leaders in today's modern age are grappling to find yet they are wandering around in the dark without a flashlight.

The challenge: breaking free of what has brought them success—sometimes immense success—to what will help them find the significance they crave in an attempt to feel alive— truly alive.

The key: understanding personal motivation and the reasons why individually, the leader might not be motivated to move to a more authentic and joyful place of leadership. Humans are intrinsically designed to better themselves when three factors are present in their environment: Autonomy, Mastery, and Connection.

We are most motivated to pursue our purpose when:

1) We are making the majority of decisions that impact our future. (Autonomy)
2) We are continually learning new skills and gaining new competence to be masterful at many things. (Mastery)
3) We are serving the community and connected to the greater good around us. (Connection)

Reflect now on your experiences as a child at play. I'm guessing you felt all three of these elements in enough balance to keep you in a state of play – or what psychologists now call "flow" – a mental state where a person is completely absorbed in a task or activity to the point, they lose track of time and themselves. Doesn't this sound like a lovely way to live life?

Remember my story from the hayloft. Autonomy, mastery and connection were readily abundant. Yet those childhood memories lie in stark contrast to how I felt navigating my 25-year corporate career.

When man gets involved, we organize structures for efficiency, but we often lose sight of the human elements of our organizations. Humans need to thrive to be self-determined and feel as though we are learning, mastering and becoming more autonomous over the decisions that affect our lives. Organized structures need efficiency to spend less and earn more. Efficiency demands adherence to rules so the company is safe—safe from downturns, risk exposure or jeopardy to the customers it's designed to serve.

This, I believe, is why it's very difficult for most individuals to thrive inside of today's organized work structures. Safety and purpose are always in tension. Corporate cultures push us to safety, yet the small voice inside pulls us toward purpose.

When clients find me, they often recount some derivation of feeling stuck. And many of the reasons they cite are because one of the elements necessary for them to thrive are missing in their environment. Some of the greatest reasons clients tell me they feel stuck are:

- They are no longer challenged by their role (not gaining new competence - Mastery).

- They dislike their boss, coworkers, or direct reports (not feeling connected - Connection).
- The culture around them is toxic (they don't feel they can make decisions that will enable a better future - Autonomy).

The list of grievances goes on and on, but most of the reasons people aren't moving to where they want to be is because one or multiple of these factors aren't being met in their life.

I'm guessing if you've read this far, you're nodding your head and thinking, "YES! This is it!   But, how do I get to this place you describe?"

This concept is easy to agree with and yet difficult to create. Remember you are a human being. And not a human doing. So, this isn't something you can just put a development plan in place for and go execute. That would be more of what you've already been good at.

This journey requires a different approach – to shift your being and create the future YOU long to see. A future filled with autonomy, mastery, and connection. And while many are interested, only a few will be able to stomach this adventure. This is **The Adventure Within**. For the previous chapters of your life, you've been building your sense of identity, that image of self you hold so dear and which has allowed you to feel safe and stable. To gain a sense of control over your own life and to disrupt that identity means you'll be disrupting the very element that has allowed you to feel in control.   However, the reason that many people turn away is because this disruption awakens the Belief Bullies and the Dream Demons. They scream loudly warning you of the dangers ahead and warning you of the thing you fear most—imminent death. Their purpose—to push you back to the land of safety where you subliminally agree to survive every day and forgo the opportunity to actually thrive.

So, this adventure—The Adventure Within—is about surrendering the need to control for a much greater purpose – a need to thrive. You desire to find that flow state (maybe 'peace') in your life where you lose yourself in a state of creating what the world needs and you are uniquely equipped to create it. Some of you will say, "But I'm not creative." This isn't about painting or making music— though those are obvious expressions of creativity. This is also about creating something that impacts the world and the people in it. Maybe a new way to serve customers, maybe a different way of operating in your business that improves connections for others, maybe it's about investing into the lives of people less advantaged than you so they can rise to new heights in their own life. All of that is creativity and more. Personal creativity really is bringing your unique gifts and talents to the world as only you can, while fixing a problem likely only you can see. In short, it is doing only that which you can do better than most.

How do you get to this place of creativity? Of solving the hard nagging problem that you've shied away from thus far? You shift your being. Stop reacting to the world around you and start standing in the center of your choices. You stop seeing the world as something that acts on you, and you become a person who can act back on the structures and systems around you in pursuit of your destiny.

What will help you as you start this adventure? I advise you to answer the following questions related to the very elements that help us become more motivated to self-author. Autonomy. Mastery. Connection.

- Do you feel 100% in control of making the decisions that impact your future?
- Are you able to learn new skills? (Even skills like emotional intelligence or "soft skills" that come at the expense of you

disrupting how you relate and show up in the world currently?)

- Are you willing to curate the connections around you that will help you find belonging, providing stability and encouragement for this long and winding adventure as you see people who are all in phases of this adventure themselves?

I don't want to be reductionist about this. Your thriving can't be reduced to three words or three bullet points. There is a lifetime of experience you've accumulated thus far, which has shaped your very self-image. So, it's likely going to be longer than three words or three months for you to shift to a place where you are fully in thriving mode.

Through my own *Adventure Within*, it became evident that my life's purpose is to help people journey through their own *Adventure Within*. I would love to work with each of you individually and help you see what happens when you're facing the question of your purpose as Susan and Mike did in our story.

The clients behind these characters are truly living a life with no regrets now and are embracing all of their experiences (painful ones included) as valuable to shape them into the leaders they are today.

However, there are also leaders like Scott who became scared, frustrated and overwhelmed. The *Adventure Within*—once illuminated—becomes so threatening to their sense of safety, they are not able to step toward purpose and a more meaningful way of leading.

Maybe you've stopped and started this adventure more times than you care to recall. You let the Belief Bullies and the Dream Demons set in and pay rent in your head. But there is hope. At some point, when the pain of staying the same becomes greater than the pain of change, **The Adventure Within** awaits. And as you live more life, I can guarantee you will encounter MORE pain, not less. And in those painful moments, your purpose—and that annoying inner voice—won't leave no matter how much alcohol, late nights at the office, or beach vacations you throw at it. It will not be numbed away.

"If you're not dead, you're not done" has become one of my favorite phrases. It has gotten me through some dark places and helped me have grace for some of those "difficult to love" people I've encountered along the journey. After all, we are all learning to live this life for the first time, together.

Your purpose only dies when you do. Yet if you allow yourself to make the shift, your legacy will live on forever through the relationships and impact you've made, and the systems or structures you've transformed.

> **But there is hope. At some point, when the pain of staying the same becomes greater than the pain of change, *The Adventure Within* awaits.**

Most of my clients will work with me for over a year as they take this journey. And to your benefit, I've been able to collect some of the best practices which I call "Power Moves" to help you start working on your being and remove focus from your doing.

You can find these best practices by scanning here:

SCAN ME

Maybe these will jumpstart your adventure. And if you find you need more assistance in the journey, please schedule a Conjunction Call with me, and we'll find the right path for you to begin your own Adventure Within. **Send me an email** ... let me know what part of the adventure you're on. I can't wait to hear from you. (jim@conjunctionleadership.com ... and yes, really that is my email address).

Until then, happy traveling. And know you can always reach out when the path gets too rough to travel alone.

– **Jim**

www.ingramcontent.com/pod-product-compliance
Lightning Source LLC
Chambersburg PA
CBHW051536120626
46551CB00012B/1250